THE LIVES AND

TIMES OF

JOHN GARZIA

THE LIVES AND TIMES OF JOHN GARZIA

Billy E. Jones

Lorraine Hale Robinson, editor

Copyright 2005 by Billy E. Jones

Published in the United States by
Teach's Cove Publishers
310 Teach's Cove Road
Bath, North Carolina 27808

All rights reserved. Unauthorized reproduction, except for brief passages in reviews, is prohibited.
First Edition

Printed by Accu Copy
Greenville, North Carolina

Library of Congress Control Number: 2004097992

ISBN: 0-9762619-0-1

Edited by Lorraine Hale Robinson

Dedicated to the memory of

John Oden

Contents

List of Illustrations	X
Preface	XII
Introduction	1
Spain	3
Ireland	7
John Garzia, the Anglican Priest	37
Colonial Virginia	39
Colonial North Carolina	53
Religion in Colonial North Carolina	59
Bath Town	85
Epilogue	117
Appendices	123
Notes	143
Works Cited...	153

List of Illustrations

Map of Northern Neck Region of Colonial Virginia . 41

Map of Colonial North Carolina........................ 55

Early Plan of Bath Town................................. 88

Saint Thomas Church, Bath............................. 92

The Garzia Chalice... 110

Preface

This monograph is the result of a task assigned to me by the St. Thomas Episcopal Church Tri-centennial Committee. The committee is responsible for the organization of St. Thomas's participation in the 2005 celebration of the tri-centennial of the town of Bath, North Carolina. My assignment was to gather information concerning the first rector of St. Thomas Church, the Reverend John Garzia. I discovered early in my research that American and Irish authors have not realized that the man who they are writing about, John Garzia of Ireland (and earlier of Spain) and John Garzia of colonial North Carolina, are the same individual. Furthermore, the accounts of this man are much more interesting and colorful when seen as a whole. Therefore the histories of John Garzia's life and times are brought together here.

The Modern Language Association method of citations and endnotes has been used in this work. The endnotes are grouped according to each section heading. An appendix has been added in order to present the full text of some pertinent documents that were in the main text necessarily summarized because of their length. Wherever possible, original manuscripts or early published editions have been used. Quotations, therefore, retain capitalization, spelling, and punctuation, and the use of *sic* has deliberately been avoided as interruptive to the flow of the text.

If this account has any merit, it is due to my fortune in having the generous assistance of many individuals, most especially my talented editor, Professor Lorraine Hale Robinson, Department of English, East Carolina University. Her intelligence and experience were invaluable in the preparation of this manuscript. Thanks are also due to John Oden, who was a real historian and talented researcher who reviewed my manuscript and introduced me to research at the North Carolina State Archives. I am also indebted to Josephine Hookway; my son, Alan Jones; my daughter, Marjorie Dannenfelser; and my wife, Hansy Jones for their reading of the manuscript and for their suggestions.

Many thanks also to the following individuals whom I have yet to meet face to face. Their assistance through correspondence, chiefly email, has been extremely beneficial. Especially valuable assistance was generously given by Mr. Bernard Canavan, a lecturer, book reviewer and illustrator in London, England; the Reverend Michael Malone, an Episcopal priest and historian in Farnham, Virginia; and Irish friends of a friend, Brendan McKenna, and his daughter Jillian McKenna. I am also grateful to Mr. Alexander Baron, a professional researcher in London, England.

B.E.J.
Bath, North Carolina
December 3, 2003

Introduction

History books tell the story of two different individuals named John Garzia. One was a Spanish priest who, to escape the attention of the Inquisition, moved to Ireland. Irish histories of the time give a fascinating account of Garzia, a man who renounced his church and Roman Catholic faith and became an infamous priestcatcher in Dublin. The other John Garzia is found in colonial American histories. This Garzia's activities centered in Bath, a village in eastern North Carolina, where religion had been all but abandoned by most settlers. Colonial accounts of Garzia tell of an uncommonly faithful and steadfast priest of the Church of England who presided in St. Thomas Parish during the building of Bath Town's St. Thomas Church.

In fact, these two characters are the same remarkable man, the Reverend John Garzia; and in this monograph his histories are joined here for the first time. The contrasting periods in the life of John Garzia serve to remind us that, given a second chance, rogues may become saints.

Spain

John Garzia was born around 1690. He was "a Native of Spain, and was bredd up A popish priest" (McGrath 506). There is evidence that his family lived in the bustling port of Cadiz (Burke 222). Garzia's family, if not wealthy, was sufficiently well off that his mother, who was undoubtedly proud of her son, was able to provide him with an allowance to help with his support. We find also that as a young priest he had sufficient means to travel. For example, during a trial, later in life, Garzia mentioned his presence in Civita Vecchia, Italy[1] in the year 1710 (McGrath 499).

During Garzia's childhood which marked the beginning of the eighteenth century, Spain was experiencing social, economic, and political problems. In the course of the previous century, the once-mighty Spanish empire had suffered the combined humiliating effects of military defeat and a devastating commercial decline. The country was burdened by oppressive religious rigidity under a series of pious but weak (and in some instances, mentally incompetent) Habsburgo (the Spanish spelling of Habsburg/Hapsburg) rulers. Both the territories and the global vision of the sixteenth century Spanish colossus which had developed under the administrations of Ferdinand and Isabella (1479-1516) and later, under Holy Roman Emperor Charles V (1516-1556) and his son Philip II (1556-1598) were lost. A century of increasing moral degeneration, extravagance and depravity peaked during John Garzia's childhood (McKendrick 125). Melveena McKendrick maintains that excesses of behavior developed not only in the life of the royal court but throughout Spanish society, most especially in the capital. Laws intended to improve public morals, such as the prohibition against riding in carriages with the curtains closed and the rule that only near relative male companions were allowed to accompany a woman when she rode in a carriage, were ignored. Respectable women, therefore, often secluded themselves lest their innocent pursuits cause them to be confused with their less virtuous sisters — of whom there were many: by the middle of the seventeenth century there were eight hundred all-night brothels in Madrid alone.

Ripples of scandal touched even the very great. The surface of social respectability had been violently agitated by the revelation of a series of liaisons between aristocratic women of the highest eminence and their male servants, and in 1641 three grandees were banished for scaling the walls of the Retiro (royal palace) at night to make love to women serving at the court as maids of honor. The monarch himself, Philip VI, was a libertine tormented by crises of guilt that drove him to establish an extraordinary relationship with a nun, Sor [Sister] Maria de 'Agreda, to whom he confessed his faults in a series of letters. However, his correspondence with and confessions to her did not prevent the king from fathering, upon his various mistresses, at least thirty illegitimate children (McKendrick126).

In this setting of simultaneous moral decay and ecclesiastic rigidity, young Father Garzia initially officiated; however, he must have soon rebelled and the Inquisition took notice. He reportedly said something that was brought to the attention of the Spanish Inquisition, and he had to escape, forsaking his homeland and family forever (Burke 221).

The background for Garzia's departure dates to the late fifteenth century. In 1478, with the Pope's permission, Isabella had acceded to the wishes of the Roman Catholic Church hierarchy and introduced the Spanish Inquisition. She intended the Inquisition as a means of guiding back to active life those *conversos* (newly converted Christians as opposed to "Old Christians") who had lapsed into their former religious practices. In time, however, the Spanish Inquisition would develop into a governmental agency that was controlled by and answerable directly to the Crown and which advanced its agenda through widespread and terrifying anonymous accusations. By the beginning of the eighteenth century, the Inquisition had developed a well-deserved reputation for cruelty, horror, and refinement of torture (McKendrick 49).

The Spanish Inquisition dramatically changed the course of Father John Garzia's life. Its attention caused him to leave a comfortable and honored position in Catholic Spain, and go to a Protestant country where, on the contrary, political and religious abuse of Roman Catholics was governmental policy. Garzia was forced to flee for his life, initially to England and from there to Ireland in 1717. Protestant Archbishop Edward Synge of the Archdiocese of Tuam (Ireland) revealed the reason for John Garzia's move when Synge informed the Archbishop of Canterbury that Garzia had spoken too freely concerning some points of Catholic dogma and as a result had been brought to the notice of the Inquisition (McGrath 508).

Ireland

Why Ireland? No doubt, if his situation had allowed it, the Rev. Garzia would have opted for a Roman Catholic state such as Italy or France. But he fled to Protestant Ireland where every effort was being made to make life unbearable for "papist" priests. To make matters worse, he understood little if any English. It is reasonable, therefore, to conclude that the offence that brought Father Garzia to the attention of the Spanish Inquisition was sufficiently egregious that he dare not remain within official reach of the Roman Catholic hierarchy. There is a second (although less likely) possibility that he was actually sent to Ireland by the Spanish church — either to get him out of the way or as part of an ongoing effort by the Roman Catholic church to aid its beset Irish branch. Indeed, after the Reformation, cordial, if secret, relations had been maintained between Spanish Catholics and the underground Catholic faithful in Ireland. According to Emily Hahn, because the Roman Catholic faith was officially outlawed in Great Britain, many Irish Priests had taken refuge in academies and schools in Spain, and Spanish priests, in spite of the very real dangers involved, often visited Ireland (99). Hahn adds that all this movement necessarily had to be under cover and out of official Protestant sight (135). Whatever his reasons, in 1717 John Garzia fled to Ireland.

The Church of Ireland (the Irish branch of the Anglican church) was established as the official state religion in Ireland, however its Anglican members were a minority of the total population: about eighty percent of the population (which owned less than one-third of the land) was Roman Catholic. Despite drastic efforts to induce them to convert, the majority of the Irish had remained Roman Catholic, no matter what their origins — whether native Irish, descendents of Norse settlers, or earlier British colonists.

To better understand John Garzia's actions in Dublin it is essential to be aware of the political and religious climate in colonial Ireland during the first quarter of the eighteenth century. In her examination of this period, Emily Hahn states that early in its history, the power of the Irish parliament was severely limited by Poyning's Law of 1495. This act stated that all legislation proposed by the Irish parliament had to be submitted to the English government for approval prior even to being *discussed* in Dublin. A second provision stipulated that all members of both Houses of Parliament in Dublin must be members of the Church of Ireland. Since all male citizens eligible to vote also had to be members of the Church of Ireland and freeholders, the number of voters was very limited.

The Irish parliament was, in fact, little more than an Anglican oligarchy and most Members of Parliament (MPs) were landowners or the sons of the peerage (179). Hahn further states that in 1559, under Queen Elizabeth I, the English Parliament passed the Act of Supremacy making the English monarch the head of the Anglican church. Later the Irish Parliament also passed a similar Act of Supremacy and the Act of Uniformity: all public officials were required to subscribe to the Oath of Supremacy. The Act of Uniformity prohibited the Roman Catholic Mass altogether and required the use of the Book of Common

Prayer. Individuals who refused to take the Oath of Supremacy were dismissed from office (133), and according to the Act of Uniformity, those who refused to attend Protestant services were fined one shilling for each offence (176).

After the Protestant Reformation in Germany, many European nations passed laws penalizing minority populations' religious beliefs, but Ireland was unique — the religion being penalized was that of the majority of the population (Hahn 182). Between 1689 and 1714, the Irish parliament passed a series of laws that further penalized Catholics. Though these "Penal Laws" or "Popery Laws" were meant to finish eradicating Catholicism in Ireland, they were not based solely on religious motives. More often these laws resulted from the desire of the English to possess additional Irish land and reflected the contempt of a ruling class for its subjects. (It is interesting to observe that laws directly affecting only Catholic *religious* practices were frequently overlooked by magistrates, whereas those that tended to promote *land confiscation* were more uniformly and enthusiastically enforced [Hahn 181-89].)

One of the first penal laws was titled the Act for the Better Securing of the Government against Papists. Under this law, no Catholic could have any "gun, pistol, or sword, or any other weapon of offense or defense, under penalty of fine, imprisonment, pillory or public whipping." The law further stated that any magistrate could appear at any time at the home of any Irish resident and search for weapons. Other penal laws forbade the celebration of the Roman Catholic Mass, and still other laws prohibited Roman Catholics from being teachers or lawyers and from holding public office. Roman Catholics could not live in an incorporated town or within a distance of five miles from one, and they could not own a horse worth more than five pounds. Catholics could not buy or lease land, and they could not receive a gift or inherit land from a Protestant. Catholics could not rent out any land worth more than thirty shillings, be the guardian of a child, or send their children abroad for an education. Inheritance laws reversed primogeniture and stipulated that the few Catholics who still owned land had to divide the land equally among all sons in the family (Laws).

The circa 1697 "Act for Banishing All Papists Exercising Any Ecclesiastical Jurisdiction, and Regulars of the Popish Clergy, Out of this Kingdom" (also called "The Bishops' Banishment Act") required all Popish clergy to leave Ireland by May 1, 1698, under the penalty of transportation (indentured servitude) for life. The law further stated that if banished persons returned, they would be hanged, drawn, and quartered. In 1704 an act required each of the priests remaining in Ireland to go to his local court and register, giving his name, age, and other particulars. At the time of this registration, the priest was also required to take an Oath of Loyalty to the Crown (Hahn 172).

Into this intensely anti-Catholic milieu came John Garzia. Instead of the favored status Garzia had known in Spain, he now was a Roman Catholic priest in a society where a majority of the population, because of its adherence to Roman Catholicism, experienced brutal religious and economic repression by its Protestant rulers. The Irish complained that they were taxed more than they could stand and without their consent, and that they were required to lodge and feed troops and provide stabling and feed for the troops' horses. These and other laws such as the prohibition of ownership of arms, the conduct (without just cause) of searches, the promulgation of tariffs and trade restrictions for the protection of English interests, and the establishment of a tax-supported state religion were the source of bitter resentment and encouraged a spirit of rebellion in Ireland. Perhaps it was the temptation of easy wealth provided by the Penal Act of 1709 that caused John Garzia to become one of the most despised persons in the history of eighteenth century Ireland. The act declared that anyone turning over to the law an unregistered priest was to receive an award of £20. Additionally £50 was offered for upper level clergy such as bishops and archbishops who exercised Roman Catholic ecclesiastical jurisdiction. The Penal Act also required that, on pain of banishment, registered priests take the Oath of Abjuration.[1] This oath meant abandoning all Roman Catholic religious loyalties and accepting the Protestant political regime that ruled Ireland. Only 33 of 1089 priests were willing to take this oath, and the refusal by the rest of them was actually what saved them. Hahn points out that to eject over a thousand priests from Ireland undoubtedly would have caused Catholic allies of the British crown to protest and possibly intervene militarily. Consequently the priests who refused to take the Oath of Abjuration were not banished; however, as a result of their non-compliance, they were designated as outlaws (185).

    The rewards that the Penal Act of 1709 offered for informing on and participating in the conviction of unregistered priests, friars, and ecclesiastical authorities induced some in Ireland to engage in the activity of "priest-catcher," but public opinion generally did not favor this new enterprise. Priest-catchers were in danger of their lives from Catholic mobs, and even many Protestants disapproved of the activities of the priest-catchers.

Priest-catchers added new terrors to the activities of Ireland's Roman Catholic clergy. Dr. Hugh MacMahon, a Roman Catholic bishop in northern Ireland described the situation:
> When our priests were confronted with greater dangers and were mercilessly pursued by government, some in order to prevent being identified by any in the congregation celebrated mass with veiled faces, others again shut themselves into a closet with the mass server alone and apertures were made or a small hole by means of which the people outside could hear the voice of the celebrant but could not recognize it, or at all events could not see him (Burke 220).

Priest-catchers themselves were in a dangerous profession. The following is excerpted from a letter from Archbishop William King, the Protestant Archbishop of Dublin to the Archbishop of Canterbury. Archbishop King, who enthusiastically promoted and encouraged priest-catchers, gave an account of the devotion of Catholics to their priests and the dangers that priest-catchers faced:
> The number of Papists is greater yn [than] of Protestants in most places 10 to one and in some 20 to one, these have all a correspondence and mutual intelligence by the means of the Priests and they can at any time bring a mob together from very remote places, and when they have set

their business, there is no more necessary but to cry a priest catcher and immediately in the open streets of Dublin you shall have a mob of 5 or 6 hundred unknown faces to fall on him, and it is well if he escape with a severe beating nay houses have been broke open to come at him (MacGrath 495).

A proclamation for the discovery of "popish rioters" issued in March 1711 by the Lord Mayor of Dublin illustrates the difficulties the authorities had to contend with in protecting priest-catchers:

Whereas on Saturday last being the 17$^{th.}$ some hundreds of the popish inhabitants of this city in a riotous and tumultuous manner assembled in Fishamble-street and in other parts of the town, in order to way-lay and insult one Henry Oxenard, on whose testimony several regulars and popish priests were lately convicted and brought to punishment in her majesty's court of Queen's Bench. And whereas the aforesaid rioters or popish mob pursued the said Oxenard thro' several streets of this city, crying out 'priest-catcher,' and whereupon threw stones, brick batts and whereupon the said Oxenard took shelter in the main guard in St. Werburgh's street. Nevertheless the said rioters pursued him tho the guard house, and insulted the guards, and afterwards wounded several constables and others, who were by the magistrates of this city sent to suppress the said tumult, and to secure the said Oxenard from the fury and insolence of the aforesaid papists (Wall 28-29).

Priest-catchers were active in many parts of the country shortly after the passage of the 1709 act, but for obvious reasons, few continued the calling for very long. There were, however two well-known professional priest-catchers who received encouragement and protection from Dublin authorities. One was Edward Tyrrell, an educated man from a prominent British family. He took up priest-hunting in 1710 in order to restore his declining economic fortunes. He traveled extensively, often with military escorts and submitted many exaggerated reports of ecclesiastics. His priest-catching ended when he was convicted of bigamy and executed in 1713. His short career as a priest-catcher did nothing to raise the profession in the public estimation (Wall 30).

The other priest-catcher sponsored by the Dublin government was none other than John Garzia. It is difficult to know, with certainty, why this priest renounced his lifelong church affiliation. Almost surely, he must have had some regrets and misgivings about this betrayal of the faith of his family and homeland. Irish historians present Garzia as a base scoundrel for his treachery. Perhaps, however, their contempt would be mollified by the knowledge of his later life as a reverent and steadfast priest of a Christian church, albeit Protestant. Those who have the advantage of a full account of his history cannot simply accept the sweeping condemnation that John Garzia was an opportunist villain. He had the courage and devotion to become, in the end, a remarkably dedicated minister of the Gospel.

There may have been some justifications, other than the promise of financial reward, for Garzia's somewhat naïve and uninformed acceptance of the promises and reliability of the Irish government. First, there was the dogma dispute that caused him to come under the scrutiny of the Spanish Inquisition. This early conflict might have concerned the celibacy rule and his desire for a legitimate marriage. It is conceivable that John Garzia already knew his future wife, Mary, as a result of previous travels and that he moved to Ireland to join her.

Another possible motive for Garzia's becoming a priest-catcher was the genuine threat of starvation. Poverty was commonplace then among Irish Catholics, but Garzia's case must have been extreme. Though he participated in Roman Catholic ecclesiastical activities for a few months after he arrived in Dublin, there is no suggestion that he had meaningful employment. He was a newly arrived Catholic foreigner who had considerable difficulty with the English language, so it is unlikely that he could easily support himself. Life was hard enough for those outlawed Irish Roman Catholic Priests who were sustained by their generally poor congregations, but Garzia's situation must have been desperate and without any hope of improvement.

At that time in Dublin, clandestine celebrations of the Roman Catholic Mass were conducted regularly and usually without interference. Roman Catholic worship, though illegal, was generally ignored by government officials. MacGrath relates that for about six months, the newly arrived Spanish priest, Father John Garzia, mixed freely with the Catholic clergy, and he attended mass at many locations in Dublin. Thus armed with information, he proceeded to Dublin Castle[2] and informed on several priests and nuns. On Sunday June 1, 1718, at around two o'clock in the morning, several priests' residences were raided. (Had the roundup occurred during daytime, the priests would likely have been rescued by Catholic mobs.) Doctor Edmund Byrne, the Roman Catholic Archbishop of Dublin; a parish priest; three Franciscans; a Jesuit; and an Augustinian[3] were arrested and then released on bail the following day (McGrath 496).

MacGrath adds that a fortnight later, on the fourteenth of June, the Convent of Poor Clares, North King Street, Dublin, was descended upon at four in the morning. Before responding to the commotion at their door, the mother abbess instructed her community to don the apparel worn by the pensioners of the convent. The officials smashed the grille and threw a cordon around the house to prevent people from coming to the assistance of the nuns, and four nuns were conveyed in carriages to the home of a local Judge [Caulfield] for processing (498).

Of the seven clergy arrested at the beginning of June, five had not chosen to register in compliance with the previously mentioned Penal Law of 1704. Archbishop Byrne and the Franciscan, Father Anthony Bryan, were registered, and they were tried separately at later dates. The unregistered priests were tried on November 7, 1718, with John Garzia appearing as a Crown witness. An interpreter was required for Garzia, and he is mistakenly described in the official proceedings as Italian. (The trial of the nuns did not occur until February 6, 1719, and that account follows later.) The following anonymous account which was printed in Dublin and was later sent by Garzia to Archbishop of Canterbury, William Wake (1657-1737), gives a fascinating first-hand description of the trial of the five unregistered priests:

An Account of the Tryals
Examinations and Convictions of
Simeon *alias* James Dillon, Francis Moor, *alias* Morray, Francis Jones *alia*s White, Michael Murphy, John Brown, all Roman Clergymen, who were Try'd at the King's Bench the 7th Day of November, 1718.

The Court being Sat and the Jury Sworn, the said several Persons being put to the bar, the first Tryal that came on was that of Mr. Dillons, and the evidence against him being one John Garsee, an Italian, who being sworn said, that about a Year ago he became acquainted with the said Dillon, and that he knew him to be a Popish priest, and the Court ask'd the said Garsee, how he could tell, that he made answer that he seen the said Dillon celebrating Mass in St. Francis Street Chappel in the usual Habit or Robes of a Priest, and several other plain remarkable Circumstances, all which being against the Laws of this Kingdom, the said Dillon being not Registered, he was immediately brought guilty.

The second Tryal was that of the said Jones, alias White, and the said Garsee being sworn, he said that about 12 or 13 Months ago he became acquainted with the said Jones, alias White, and that he knew him to be a Franciscan Fryar, the court ask'd him how they became acquainted the Witness said that they Lodg'd in the same

House together for Four Months, the Court Examin'd the said Garsee how he could tell that the said Jones was a Franciscan Fryer, who answer'd that the said Jones, alias White himself told him so and besides that there was a certain sort of a Prayer that belong'd to that Order, which the said Jones alias White frequently used, upon which the said Jones, alias White having no Defense to make for himself and the Witness having Sworn that he seen him Celebrate Mass in Doctor Naries Chappel in the usual Habit or Robes, and at several other Places, the said Jones, alias White, was also immediately found Guilty, having remained in the Kingdom contrary to Law.

The third Tryal was that of Francis Moore alias Morry, and the same Witness being Sworn against him, he said that he became acquainted with him about fourteen Months ago, and that he very well knew him to be a Franciscan Fryar, and to have Celebrated Mass very often in Cook Street and for the Nunns at the Dutchess of Tyrconnels, how he could tell that the Traverser [defendant] was a Franciscan Fryer, that he told him so himself and besides he told him that he lately came out of Bilboa in Spain, the said Moore alias Morry being ask'd by the court if he had anything to say for himself, he said that there was one Denis Ryan in Court who lock'd and unlock'd the Chappel Door in

Cook Street, could make Oath that he the said Moore alias Moory did not Celebrate Mass in the said Chappel for 15 Months before the said Ryan being called, and Sworn in the behalf of the Traverser, he upon his Oath being Cross Examin'd and did not rightly behave himself, he was ordered by the court to be put into the Dock, and without any more ado, the Jury brought the said Moore alias Morry in Guilty, having Officiated contrary to Law.

The 4th Tryal that came on, was that of Michael Murpheys the said Garsee being Sworn he said, that he very well knew Murpheys to be a Priest and Jesuite for that he seen him often Celebrate Mass in the usual Habit and Robes of a Priest, and after the usual Testimony, The court ask'd him how he could tell, that the said Murphy was a Jesuite, who answer'd that the said Murphy told him so (and further) that when Garsee told him he was going to Portugal, that he said Murphy writ several Letters by him to other Jesuits there and said that the said Murphy kept School in Dublin, taught Grammar and Philosophy: The Court ask'd Murphy what he had to say for himself, who desir'd the Court to ask the said Garsee what he did with the Letters that he gave him to carry to Portugal or why he had not them to Produce against him in Court, which the Court asking, the said Garsee said that he gave 'em to the

Duke of Bolton in December last, the said Murphy having no other Defense to make for himself, he was upon sight brought in Guilty. The Fifth and last Tryal that came on was that of John Browne, and the said Garsee being sworn for the King, he upon Oath said that he knew the said Brown to be an Augustinian Fryar, and that on the 28 th of August last was a Twelve Month He seen him Celebrate Mass in the Chappel of the Augustinians in St. John's Lane. The Court asked him how long he had known the Traverser, who answered that it was about Eight Years ago, since he seen him at a Place called Civila Vactia in Italy, the Court ask'd him how he came to know Mr. Brown in Dublin, the Witness answered that it was the Traverser that knew and Challeng'd him first, and that by his Discourse with him he was full sensible that he was the Self Same Man he seen in Italy, the Court asked him how he could tell that he was an Augustinian Fryer, who answered that the Traverser himself told him so. Dublin Printed in the Year 1718 (Wake Letters 13: 43).

As was mentioned, Archbishop William Byrne and the Franciscan Father Anthony Bryan had registered as the law prescribed and for that reason were charged separately. Bryan's trial was conducted in late November 1718. He was charged only with celebrating mass out of the parish for which he was registered. Garzia appeared as a witness for the prosecution and swore that he had seen the priest celebrate mass on several occasions and furthermore had attended a service during which Bryan preached a sermon. Bryan was found guilty and was sentenced to be imprisoned until he could be transported out of His Majesty's dominions. In his spirited defense, Bryan stated that Garzia was a Jew who only pretended to be a priest. This description was likely the source of later references to Garzia as a "Spanish Jew" (MacGrath 502) and a "Portuguese Jew" (Burke 220). There appears to be ample evidence that this characterization of Garzia by Bryan resulted from contempt rather than fact and that "Jew" was meant as a general term of derision. Even his detractors among Catholic historians such as Wall and MacGrath accept the fact that John Garzia was not Jewish but was an ordained Spanish priest. MacGrath, who was no admirer of Garzia, summed up the evidence for Garzia having been a priest as follows: "his intimate acquaintance with Catholic ritual and the facility with which he imposed on the archbishop and his priests, and his statements at a later date that he had lodged in the same house as Francis Jones *alias* White for four months (probably at the friary of Adam and Eve's, (Dublin) and that he had been accosted by John Browne whom he had known eight years before that in Civita Vecchia would tend to support his frequently-repeated claim that he (Garzia) had been ordained a Catholic priest" (596).

    Whether any of the six convicted priests were actually transported to Spain is not recorded. War broke out between England and Spain and was proclaimed in Dublin in 1718; accordingly, all traffic between Ireland and Spain was suspended. It is known that later, other priests who had already been transported adopted fictitious names and returned from Spain without molestation. MacGrath suggests that the same may be true for these six convicted priests (500).

Archbishop Byrne's trial was put off and did not occur until a year after the other clergy were convicted. Byrne was charged with adopting the title of and officiating as Archbishop of Dublin. In addition he was accused of celebrating mass outside of the parish in which he was registered. When John Garzia was called on to testify, he did not appear, possibly as a result of an official order by the Irish government. There being no witness for the prosecution, the jury returned a verdict of not guilty.

Byrne was immediately released. This is remarkable in view of two proclamations issued that year that strictly enjoined magistrates to arrest all Catholic archbishops, bishops, vicars-general, and regulars because of a threatened invasion from Spain. According to MacGrath, the acquittal of the Archbishop was probably due in a large measure to the intervention of one of the Catholic monarchs of Europe. "It was usual for the ambassadors of Catholic powers in London to intercede in such cases: in return, British envoys to Catholic countries commonly intervened in behalf of persecuted Protestant subjects." Upon his release, the Archbishop resumed his functions without official interference (502).

At about the time of his participation in the arrest of the priests and nuns, John Garzia was married. We know little of his wife Mary's origins, but she must have been from the Dublin vicinity and, without doubt, was Protestant.

On February 6, 1719, four nuns — Anne Crawford, Mary Smith, Jane Sexton, and Mary Chivers — were tried, and once again John Garzia was the leading witness. A printed contemporary account with its fascinating detail which was sent by Garzia to Archbishop Wake survives among Archbishop Wake's letters (see Appendix A). Apparently these women's only offense was that they were practicing nuns. Garzia's name is misspelled as it was in the first trial account, but the spelling is phonetically similar to the Spanish pronunciation of Garzia. The narrator tells us that Garzia could "speak no English" and needed an interpreter in court. This explains the statements in both trial accounts that defendants and their councils "desired that Garzia be examined."

When, during the course of the trial, Garzia was asked how he knew the defendants to be nuns. He answered "that he was sensible that every young Woman who took the Vow of Chasity, and became a Nunn, had in a year's time a Ring bestowed upon her, and a knotted Cord, called a St. Francis's Girdle" and that he knew every one of the "traversers [defendants] to have the like." He also testified that he "likewise knew them severally to have used a prayer that is not used by others but such as are Nuns" and that they wore nun's habits when at home but "when they came abroad, they left that Black and White at Hom . . . for fear of being discovered." Garzia further testified that one of the nuns, Anne Crawford "was an Abbiss and so Reputed and Respected by all the rest, and that all the rest of the Gentlewomen call'd her Mother."

Another witness in the Nun's trial was Mrs. George Sergeant, wife of the High Constable of Dublin. Mrs. Sergeant had searched the nuns after their capture and had discovered "a pair of Beads and a Ring in Mrs. Smith's Pocket and that she likewise found a knotted

Cord about her Body on the outside of her Shift; and that she found another pair of beads, a prayer book and a small crucifix in the said Mrs. Sexton's Pocket, and another Cord about her Body on the outside of her Shift; but that she found nothing with the other two." Mrs. Sergeant produced the "aforesaid things in Court, which were view'd by the judges and several others."

After various witnesses had testified, "the Court ask'd the Traversers what they had to say for themselves, or if they had any Witnesses to produce, the said Crafford said that Garsee Swore against her, but was false as God is true, but they had no Witnesses but God Almighty." The jury "having received the charge, brought in their Verdict, that the said Mrs. Smith and Sexton were Guilty, and the other two not Guilty . . . Smith and Sexton are to be transported."

When the trial was over "the said Garsee went off well guarded by one of the Messengers, a Sergeant and 10 soldiers" (Wake Letters 13: 42-44).

However, the nuns were not transported after all. According to MacGrath, it was realized during the course of these events that women were not subject to any Penal Laws; therefore the nuns were released (498).

With the conviction of the six priests, Garzia had fulfilled the reward provisions of the Penal Act of 1709. However four months after the conviction of the first five priests, he not only had *not* received any of the promised reward, but he was also experiencing the wrath of Catholic mobs. On March 3, 1719, he wrote to claim his reward with the following petition to the Lords Justices:

    To theire Excellencys the Lords Justices and Council of Ireland
    The humble Petition of John Garzia.

Sheweth,

That your Petitioner by Act of Parliament has Informed and were found Guilty the severall undernamed Priests in the Citty of Dublin as non Registered Priests, Simeon Dillon, a seculiar Priest, Francis Jones alias White a Francisscon Fryer, Francis Moore, Alias Morrey a Francisscon Fryer, John Browne and Augustine Fryer, Michaell Murphy a Jessuit, and Anthony Brien who is likewise Convicted tho' registered but did not take the Oaths, being in Dispute as yett.

That your Petitioner's Reward According to Act of Parliam^t for the first five priests above Mentioned was one hundred pounds of Which your Petitioner has not received a peny being a stranger to Such Demand, and knows not who to apply for the Same other then to your Excell^{ies} and honn^{rs}.

That your pet^r. Has noe manner of Way of getting being an Actuall Stranger in this Kingdome, Sometime in June last had the hon^r of Receiveing a present by theire Exc^{ies}. ord^{rs}. off ffifty pounds, your pet^r. haveing a family to Maintaine and himselfe lyeing Sick for a considerable time under the Doctr^s hands which Misfortunes Consumed the s^d Present in a short time, That yor Pet$^{r\text{-}}$ dare not walke the Streetes about his business being in Danger of his life by the Romans.

May it therefore please yor Ex^{cies} and Hon^{rs} to grant your Pet^r yor Propper ord^r for to receive the Same Reward of a hundred pounds as y^t in case of Delay of time for raiseing the Same to grant yor Pet^r some present Reliefe to wards his Maintainance as to yor Ex^{cies}: and Hon^{rs}. Seeme proper.

And yor Pet^r. will ever Pray (MacGrath 505).

At that time Garzia's "family" consisted of Garzia and his wife Mary. According to MacGrath, the foregoing petition prompted the Lords Justices to write the Lord Mayor of Dublin on Garzia's behalf. Accordingly Archbishop King himself ordered that the following letter be sent to the mayor:

Dublin
March 16th. 1718[-9]
My Lord

There are du to the bearer M^r. Garcia severall sums for the good service he hath done the Government but by the negligence of Collectors or some other impedim^t. I find he has gotten nothing, my Lord this is a very great discouragement, and will have I fear very ill consequences, we ordered m^r. Maddockes to write to your Lordship about this, which I hope he did, but I farther hope, that my sending it may have some influence and that we shall hear his mon'y is paid, which will be very gratefull to

My Lord

Your Lordsps &c.

W : D (MacGrath505)
The Lord Mayor of Dublin refused to accept responsibility for paying the reward, so Garzia appealed to the Lords Justices once again. (See Appendix B) In this letter Garzia wrote that he was a native of Spain and was "bredd up A popish priest and in that profession continued til he came into this Kingdom some Months agoe, When he was converted to the Protestant Religion." He added that he had became acquainted with most of the "Popish" clergy before he converted and that he had testified in trials against several of them but the trials of some of the priests were put off until the next court term. Garzia wrote that he had been offered bribes if he would not give further testimony but that he was not to be corrupted and that he was resolved to remain in Ireland until the trials were completed. He further wrote that the Catholics in Dublin had frequently insulted him and had "Contrived ways to take away his life, and perticulerly of fryday the 4th in a Most barbarous Maner raised a great Mobb" against him and that he had barely escaped with his Life. Further, since he was now afraid to walk the streets, he was deprived of the means of earning a living; Garzia wrote that he could move to safety in England or some other part of the Empire but that he was remaining [in Ireland] "to serve the Crown and to prosecute the said Popish Clergy." He therefore requested "some small Alowance to Maintain And Support him [your poor Pet[r]] till next terme that the said trials are over" (MacGrath 506).

This second appeal which was discussed at a meeting of the Lords Justices on March 28, 1719 finally brought relief. The Grand Jury awarded Garzia £100. He was also granted apartments in Dublin Castle, the center of the English colonial administration of Ireland (Burke 220). The Garzias moved to their new quarters and remained in Dublin Castle for the rest of their eventful life in Ireland. The relatively safe existence provided by Dublin Castle was especially beneficial for the Garzias because two of the Garzia children were born there. Daughter Katherine was born May 20, 1720, and daughter Jane was born December 17, 1721. The Garzias were provided protection from irate Catholics, and they also had more direct access to government officials.[4]

John Garzia's history would undoubtedly be much richer and perhaps better understood if more information about Mary had survived. One can only speculate on the degree of influence she had in the course of his life. Circumstances strongly suggest that she was a devout Protestant and that John met her in the vicinity of Dublin. One can imagine that Garzia's attraction to her could have been a principal reason for his conversion.

Mary remains a mystery, but a study of available copies of the originals of John's letters reveals a fascinating possibility. A letter to the Archbishop of Canterbury which was written in Latin was undoubtedly written by John. As a Roman Catholic priest, Garzia would be proficient with Latin. However all the other available letters were undoubtedly written by another hand, and they are also written in excellent English. The grammar and spelling are comparable to that of contemporary, well-educated individuals, and the texts indicate a real grasp of the subtleties of the English language. It is most unlikely that they could have been written by John whose English was so poor at that time as to require an interpreter during the trials. Frequent mention of personal details suggests strongly that an immediate family member, Mary, wrote John's letters. These letters demonstrate that, if Mary were the writer, she was an intelligent, determined, and well-educated woman who was resolutely Protestant. This description best fits a woman belonging to one of the more privileged families that had more recently arrived in Dublin from England. Unfortunately, there was a fire in the Public Record Office in Dublin in 1922, and many official records including marriages, births, deaths, wills and census data were lost. The Church of Ireland parish registers were also lost. Consequently, no authoritative information concerning Mary is available, and her influence on her husband's activities must at this time be left to informed conjecture.

On May 3, 1719, shortly after his move to Dublin Castle, Garzia openly converted to the established church. He was certified as a convert on May 5, and his name was officially entered on the rolls of the Chancellery ten days later (MacGrath 507). He was now a priest of the Church of England since ordination to the Anglican priesthood was not required for clergy who had converted from the Roman Catholic priesthood.

In November 1719 Garzia again approached the Lord Lieutenant and Council with a request for assistance. They appointed a committee to report on Garzia's case and the findings were submitted on January 14, 1720. Consistent with the Irish colonial government's record of incompetence and apparent deceit, nothing came of the request.

Garzia then made an appeal to Doctor William Wake, the Archbishop of Canterbury. This communication consisted of the previously mentioned letter in Latin which introduced the printed accounts of the trials of the

priests and nuns. To learn more, Archbishop Wake wrote Protestant Archbishop Edward Synge of the Archdiocese of Tuam (Ireland) requesting particulars concerning the priest-catcher, John Garzia. On March 6, 1720, Archbishop Synge replied:
> Upon the receipt of your Grace's letter I sent for Garzia and told him what your Grace was pleased to direct me. The man was a Romanish priest either in Spain or Portugal (I do not well remember which) from whence he made his escape for fear of the Inquisition, having (as it is said) been known to speak with some freedom concerning some points of the Romanish faith. It is above two years since he came by way of England — as I have been told — into this kingdom where for above half a year he continued to act as a priest until being further convinced he wholly renounced the Church of Rome, and for some service which he has done in discovering divers of the Romish clergy who were convicted upon his evidence, he has received some reward from the Government with liberty to lodge in the Castle of Dublin to protect him from the Insults of the Papists Burke221).

In spite of this high level exchange, the Garzias received no relief from the Archbishop of Canterbury, and their distress is manifest in their next appeal to the Lords Justices and Privy Council dated July 1720.
> To their Excellencies the Lords

Justices and the Lords of his Majesty's Privy Council.

The humble Petition of John Garcia a converted popish priest.

Sheweth That your Petitioner was a popish Priest and that he made his publicke recantation in the church of Ireland and took the oaths in the King's Bench about three years ago.

That the Irish papists did severall times endeavour to destroy your Petitioner by secret practices and open violence so that your Petitioner is in perfect fear of his life Seeing himself abused and sometimes assaulted in the streets by papists or persons disaffected to his Majesty.

That your said Petitioner knows no other reason of his being so abused but because he is become a Protestant and has informed against and has by due course of law six Irish popish priests and three nuns. That the popish clergy being incenced against your Petitioner for doing the duty of a true Protestant and faithfull subject did write to Spaine against him and have been the occasion of your Petitioner's mother and relatives having suffered persecution and that his own picture was burnt by sentence of the inquisition who would burn him alsoe if he should fall into their unmercifull hands. So that your Petitioner is deprived of the yearly assistance he received from his said mother.

That his Grace the Duke of Bolton[5] being sensible of the good services done by Your Petitioner to the Government and the Protestant religion in discovering and prosecuting the enemies of both at a very criticall juncture, did promise to settle on your petitioner a pension of £50 per annum for his and his family subsistence and your Petitioner hopes that his Excellency my Lord Chancellor will remember the truth of this last allegation.

That the said pension was not settled on your Petitioner who is actually in greate want and poverty with his wife and two children, and in danger of being arrested by those he was forced to borrow from to prevent starving.

J. Garcia.

{endorsed} That petition be referred to a Committee of the whole Board to report 1 July 1720 (Burke 221-22).

The situation had gone from bad to desperate. Garzia was facing the prospect of debtor's prison. Not only had he not received the pension payments that had been promised, but to make matters worse, the allowance from his mother had stopped. To add to his distress, Garzia's mother and other relatives in Cadiz were being punished for his flight and his betrayal of the Roman Catholic faith, therefore there was no hope of return to his homeland.

The Council granted a miserable £15, and there was no word of the promised pension. In desperation Garzia appealed to his former protector, Archbishop King of

Dublin, who sent him to Judge Boat (given name unknown) with the following letter of recommendation. Judge Boat was the same judge who had presided in one or both of the previously mentioned trials.

> My Lord
> The bearer I know has bin very servicable in Discovering priests, and has bin greatly affronted and abused on that acco^t. it is not only his case, but the fate of all those that give any assistance to put the Laws in Execution. I enclose his present circumstances as he gives them in writing, the man has not a Groat[6] in the world I verily believe and must go to Jail, I use not to trouble Judges in such cases, but I know the poor mans to be so pityable that I have ventured to go out of my way on such an extraordinary occasion how your Lordship will help him, I can't say, but I find the papists with their Mobs & insolence are too hard for all our Laws, the Bearers name is Garzia who I believe has bin before you as a witness in the Kings Bench, he seems to me an honest innocent man, I have done what I cou'd to help him, and Doubt not of your Lordships good inclination as farre as Justice will permitt you. Which is all my Lord from
> Yourr Lordships &c
> W : D (McGrath 509)

The letter saved Garzia from debtor's prison, but he gained no relief either from poverty or from the Catholic mob. On the following October 11, Garzia renewed his appeal to the Council with a repetition of his plight and the addition of the following. He is assaulted in the Castle and the streets by which reason your Petitioner has lost the libertie of walking the streets both Sundays and week days and is forced to keep his room like a prisoner for the occasion of his great persecution (Burke 222).

William Burke writes that as a result of this appeal, a committee was organized to consider Garzia's situation. The committee consisted of the Archbishop of Tuam, the Bishop of Meath, and two laymen: Benjamin Parry and James Tynte. The committee examined Garzia by oath and found that he became a Protestant in November, 1717. He had been paid £10 by the Lords Justices and £50 by the Privy council in 1718; in 1719 he received £20 from the Lord Lieutenant and £30 from the Lords Justices; in 1720 he received £15 from the Lords Justices (a total of £125). In addition the Committee reported that "the Grand Jury of the city of Dublin presented a sum of £100 for the services he had done but he knows not, he says, how much he got having paid a good part in fees and interest on money he had borrowed. But he hardly thinks £80 came to him." The Committee recommended Garzia for relief, but whatever money he received lasted only until the beginning of the next year (222).

On May 4, 1721, Garzia again appealed to the Lords Justices and Council. In his appeal Garzia's name is misspelled which supports the assumption that Mary, not John, may have been the author of this communication. The letter reveals that Garzia's mother had joined the Inquisition in Spain in wanting to burn him alive. The missive also relates that, on the arrival in the preceding year of the newly appointed viceroy to Ireland, the Garzias had been moved from their original quarters in Dublin Castle to a garret which until then had been a passageway.

Your Excellency and Lordships may see that if he troubles with frequent petitions it is not bicause he is greedy or extravagent in his expenses but bicause he is really poor and unfortunate. It is more than three years since it pleased God to call your petitioner into the Kingdom of Light. He is become the object of the rage and hatred of all papists as also of many who call them selves Protestants. He is forced to keep his chamber and never go out of the Castle except Sundays that he repair to church That perpetual confinement and the want of necessaryes for life destroys his health. His mother being informed of your Petitioner's conversion by means of the Irish papists that live in Cadiz, is so far from helping him that she would joyn with the Inquisition to burn him alive and in so doing she would believe to do God service. Your Petitioner avers that most of the money he has received has been laid out in repairing and furnishing his room and in the paying of charges of two fitts of sickness. When the late Lord Lieutenant came last, your Petitioner was putt in a garrett that had been till then a passage only, he was forced to make severall partitions at his own cost, he is actually with out bread for himself and his Poor family and is but just risen out of a purple feavor.

J. Garcia (Burke 222-23)

This letter must have produced results because the Garzias were not again heard from until the next year (1722) when, on March 19, Garzia pleaded that the long promised pension might be granted him or, if not, he might be given a church position, but neither the pension nor the benefice was granted on that occasion. Even his patron, Archbishop King was not yet prepared to admit John fully to the "cloth" (MacGrath). However, at about that time the Lords Justices "had recommended him to be one of the missionaries to be sent to Minorca" (Burke 223).[7] Later in the year Garzia repeated this appeal and the Lords Justices forwarded his request to Lord Bolton, the Lord Lieutenant who at that time was in London. The matter of what to do with the Garzias was then referred to Lord Carteret, the British Secretary of State.

Though it is not recorded, John Garzia must have gotten an attractive offer to move to England. The next evidence of him is from February 15, 1723, when he wrote the Lords Justices and Council requesting financial help for his move to London. One can imagine the rejoicing by other Dublin Castle residents. Here was a chance to permanently rid the castle of this embarrassing and expensive resident and his growing family. MacGrath writes that the response was prompt, and further that there appears to be no mention of John Garzia's later activities in Irish historical writings or Irish state correspondence (513).

John Garzia, the Anglican Priest

The history of the "other" John Garzia starts six months later in England. Like Archbishop King in Dublin, Bishop Edmund Gibson of London recognized the good qualities in John Garzia and became his sponsor and benefactor. Garzia's appreciation of the bishop's benevolence is conspicuous in Garzia's subsequent letters to London. Bishop Gibson ordered that the Reverend Mr. John Garzia was to receive the "king's bounty"[1] of £20 and that he be transported to serve the church in "Insulis Bahamid" (Bahamas).

On August 9, 1723, at Gravesend on the Thames, John and Mary, and their two young daughters boarded the *Hanover*, a ship that was being chartered by Mrs. George Phenney, the wife of the governor of the Bahamas. However, the Garzias never reached the Bahamas. In fact, they soon found themselves back in Ireland. According to the Garzia entry in William Powell's DNCB, the Garzia family was made to leave the *Hanover* at Cork because John was charged with the theft of a chalice from a Roman Catholic church where he had officiated. John was also accused of taking a box of books when he disembarked — books intended as a gift from the Bishop of London to a library at Harbor Island in the Bahamas (281-

82). But whether Garzia underwent legal action for these poorly documented allegations cannot be determined.[2]

Colonial Virginia

A few months later John had evidently resolved his difficulties in Cork. On April 8, 1724, he again received the king's bounty, and the Garzia family again boarded a ship. This time they headed for a new life in the colony of Virginia.

The Garzias arrived in the port of Norfolk without notable incidents during their long sail across the Atlantic. From Williamsburg, in a letter dated July 17, 1724, Commissary[1] James Blair informed the Bishop of London, Edmund Gibson that Governor Hugh Drysdale had, on the basis of Bishop Gibson's recommendation, sent Garzia to the Elizabeth River Parish in Lower Norfolk County although Blair also informed the bishop that Blair feared that Garzia's imperfect English might antagonize some (Manross 171). Governor Drysdale himself wrote Bishop Gibson concerning the placement of Garzia and Virginia's need for additional clergymen:

> I was honored with your Ldspps letter which was delivered to me by the reverend Mr. Garcia and in obedience to your Ldspps comands therein, I have presented him to the best parish now vacant within my Goverment, regarding him, from your Ldspps character, as a person of publick merit & deserving encouragement . . . The Colony labours under great difficulty for want of Clergymen: severall parishes lies

unsupplied, and has been in that condition years past . . . (Barten 7).

The Rev. John Garzia served as rector of Christ Church, Norfolk, during the year 1724 (Barten).[2] However, as the commissary feared, the residents of Lower Norfolk were probably unhappy with their parson's English, because the Garzias soon moved to the town of Farnham[3] in North Farnham Parish, Richmond County, Virginia (Powell 281). No doubt the parishioners in that more remote community were less inclined than their Norfolk brothers and sisters to be fastidious concerning their priest's English because Garzia served North Farnham Parish from 1725 until 1733.

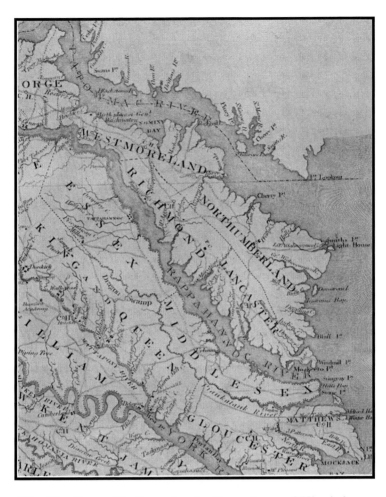

The Northern Neck region in the colony of Virginia

A portion of section 6 of the Bishop James Madison Map, *A Map of Virginia Formed from Actual Surveys,* 1818. "FC" (above the D in *Richmond)* is the location of Farnham County. Courtesy of the Library of Virginia, Richmond.

Very little is recorded concerning John Garzia's ministry in Virginia. George Brydon, a noted colonial church historian briefly gave Garzia's work favorable mention (235), and it is recorded elsewhere that Parson Garzia actively instructed and baptized slaves during his ministry in Farnham (Powell 281). He was sufficiently effective in his work as parish priest that James Blair, the Bishop of London's commissary in Williamsburg, expressed his favorable opinion of Garzia's work in the following certificate written at the behest of Governor William Gooch (Virginia Governor 1727-1749). This document was given to Garzia at the time he was being considered as a candidate by the Vestry of St. Thomas Parish in North Carolina:

Williamsburgh Mar. 17, 1732-3.
(In the endnotes see note number 1 for the appendix section.)
Whereas the Reverend Mr. John Garcia dessyning to remove himself and his family into North-Carolina is desirous of a Certificate from me of his life and Conversation during his continuance in this Country of Virginia; These are to certify to all persons concerned that during the time of his Ministry in this Government (which is now near nine years) as far as I know he has been a person of a good life and conversation, and sober and diligent in the Exercise of his Ministerial function.

James Blair, Commissary.
Wmsburgh June 27th 1733

The above Certificate is given to Mr. Garzia by the Bishop of London's Commissary William Gooch (Cain 341).

Parson Garzia's ministry evidently flourished in Virginia, and his family also developed. Three more children were born during the nine years the Garzias lived in Virginia. Their third child, Mary, who was probably born in Norfolk, died in Farnham October 1725. The next child, Anne, who was born in Farnham on November 1, 1725, died at the age of three. The fifth and last child, John, was born in Farnham September 28, 1731 (King 66). [4]

Though there is very little documentation of the Garzia family's life in Virginia, there is one fascinating source, namely the Richmond County court records. John Garzia was no stranger to these courts, and the records of these court proceedings (Sparacio) provide a decidedly more personal view of John Garzia than is found elsewhere. The records of John Garzia's court appearances suggest that the Garzias lived well beyond their means in Virginia. The Richmond County court records show many actions against Garzia for substantial debt. There is no evidence that Garzia did not receive his clerical salary which was probably around the prevailing £50 annually. However, he evidently required much more than the modest salary of a country parson to maintain himself as an Anglican priest with both a family and servants to support. During the nine years Garzia was in Virginia, there were no less than eight cases in which the Richmond County court issued orders concerning his debts. Two of these cases were settled in court. For instance, in 1729, after several hearings and continuances an order was issued as follows:

MITCHELL v GARZIA In an action of debt between ARCHIBALD MITCHELL, Plt. and JOHN GARZIA, Clerk. [cleric], Deft. for twelve pounds, two shillings currency or tobacco at the generall markett price[5] due by Bill both partys having last Court entred into a Rule to submit their differences to the final determination and award of JOHN TAYLOE, Gent. JOHN TAYLOE this day returned his award which is ordered to be recorded and is in these words. "I doe order and award tht the Reverend JOHN GARZIA pay to ARCHIBALD MITCHELL in satisfaction of the within Bill two two [sic] thousand four hundred twenty pounds of good and lawfull tobacco to be paid in hogsheads not under seven hundred neat, ARCHIBALD MITCHELL to pay his own costs and to take noe Execution for this Debt till the 10th day of February next ensueing this 30th th of June 1729
JOHN TAYLOE
(Sparacio. *Book 1721-1732* 473).

Two of the actions for debt against Garzia for a total value of approximately £18 were dismissed, presumably as a result of out-of-court settlements (Sparacio. *Book 1721-1732* 272, 386). Four of the actions for a total value of approximately £60 which were dated late in the year 1732, and in 1733 were also ordered dismissed, undoubtedly because Garzia had already left the province and his debts were not collectable (Sparacio. *Book 1732-1739* 17, 91,121,123).

Interestingly John Garzia himself also had to resort to the court to collect debts owed to him. The Sparacio records show that Garzia was the plaintiff in two actions of debt for a total of 2500 lbs. of tobacco, and two actions for debt for a total of £ 60. These four cases were dismissed, again presumably because they were settled out-of-court (*Book 1721-1732* 356, 380, 405, 579). Garzia also attached an estate in order to collect a debt. The case was dismissed, (in this instance, given the date, probably because Garzia had already left the province) (*Book 1732-1739* 49). However, one case concerning indebtedness to Garzia came to trial. The court ruled for Garzia, as supported by the testimony of one Charles Grymes, in a case for debt against a gentleman named Thomas Waring:

> GARZIA v WARING In an action of Case between the Reverend JOHN GARZIA, Plt. And THOMAS WARING, Gent, Deft. For four pounds, seven shillings and six pence currant money due by assumpsit the Deft. Having last November Court put in his Plea; whereupon the Cause was continued till this Court for tryall, on hearing the arguments of both partys and the Evidence of CHARLES GRYMES, Gent. On behalf of the Plt. It is the opinion of this Court that JOHN GARZIA recover of THOMAS WARING the sum of four pounds, seven shillings and six pence and that he pay the same unto him with costs of suit -and one Attorney's fee als Exo
>
> GRYMES v GARZIA CHARLES GRYMES, Gent., being summoned an

Evidence for the Reverend JOHN GARZIA Plt. Against THOMAS WARING, Gent., Deft. And making Oath that he has attended three days on the suit, it is therefore ordered that JOHN GARZIA pay him ninety pounds of tobacco for the same with costs als Exo (*Book 1721- 1732* 80).

Several years earlier, John Garzia is revealed to have had at least one of the more ordinary human failings by an order dated June 7, 1727. This order also serves to illustrate the degree of involvement by governments in the regulation of moral behavior in colonial times.

GARZIA to be summoned. Ordered the Sheriff summon to next court the Reverend John Garzia of Northfarnham Parish to answer the Presentment of the Grandjury against him for swearing one Oath the 24th day of March last by Information of MARY THORNTON, it is therefore ordered the Sheriff summon to next Court MARY THORNTON to testifye her knowledge concerning the same.

The presentment against Garzia was ordered dismissed in the next session (Sparacio *Book 1721-1732* 351, 365).

The Garzia household in Farnham had servants and many of the servant problems typical of a period where "service" took so many forms. Historian Hugh Lefler's description of colonial society suggests that, even though they were not wealthy, the Garzia family would have been considered members of the gentry "class" in colonial America. Colonial American gentry tended to be a small group of wealthier, better educated, and more influential citizens including large landowners, public officials, wealthy merchants, Anglican ministers, and professional men, such as lawyers and doctors[6] (114). If he were to maintain himself as a proper Anglican priest, Parson Garzia's home and its furnishings, the food that he served his guests, and even his dress and personal appearance would reflect his social standing. Since few of the labor-saving conveniences of modern day living existed in those days, servants were essential to maintain the homes of the gentry and to allow their owners to pursue their professional activities. So it was in the Garzia home: court records show that the Garzias had indentured servants (Sparacio. Book 1721-32 483, 613).

Indentured servants were the lowest class of the majority population in colonial America. Lefler divided this "Christian Servants" class into three main types of non-free workers: voluntary servants, involuntary servants, and apprentices. The largest was the voluntary group, the "redemptioners," who were poor people who voluntarily "bound" themselves by a written contract, or indenture, to a master for a fixed number of years, usually in order to redeem their passage from Europe to America. The second group, involuntary servants, included felons, convicted paupers, political prisoners, and others who were sentenced by British courts to terms of servitude in the colonies in lieu of more severe punishment in England. The last group was apprentices who were generally dependent orphans, illegitimate white children, and children of vagrants who were apprenticed to their "masters" until the "age of maturity" — eighteen for girls and twenty-one for boys. Lefler lists mechanic, blacksmith, carpenter, cooper, cordwainer, weaver, tailor, joiner, mariner, wheelwright, fisherman, silversmith, ditcher, and barber among the no fewer than thirty different trades noted in the North Carolina apprenticeship records (124-26). The Richmond County Court Orders reveal that there were at the least two indentured servants in the Garzia home. One was named Thomas Warrell (variously spelled: Warrell, Werrell, Worrell) (Sparacio *Book 1721-1732* 483, 566 and *Book 1732-1739* 2), and the other, Elizabeth Parsons (Sparacio *Book 1721-1732* 613, 657 and *Book 1732-1739* 8). For a period of time these two servants were employed concurrently in the Garzia home. They were well known by the courts because Garzia took them there. The turbulent relationship between these two servants and Garzia suggests that they might have been of the previously described "involuntary" rather than "voluntary" class of indentured servants.

The first recorded Richmond County court order against Thomas Warrell is dated October 1729 and concerns Warrell's running away. The offence of "having fugitively absented himself [herself] from his [her] Masters service" was commonly addressed by the Richmond County Court. The standard penalty was an addition to the period of servitude to equal twice the number of days absent. Also additional servitude time was calculated to cover in value the cost of capture and retrieval of the escaped servant.

WARRELL to serve Garzia
THOMAS WARRELL, Servant to Mr. JOHN GARZIA having fugitively absented himself from his Masters service for the space of twenty seven days and JOHN GARZIA making it appear to this Court that he expended one thousand three hundred ninety six pounds of tobacco in pro-

cureing him againe, it is therefore ordered that THOMAS WARRELL serve his Master or his assigns fifty four days for the twenty seven days absence and according to Law for the one thousand three hundred ninety six pounds of tobacco after his time by Indenture custom or otherwise is fully expired (Sparacio. *Book 1721-1732* 483).

The next recorded court order concerning Mr. Warrell, dated March 7, 1731, reveals that he and Garzia were having serious differences with one another:

WERRELL Whipt It appearing to this Court that THOMAS WERRELL, Servant to JOHN GARZIA, did threaten to kill his Master, it is therefore ordered that for the Offence the Sheriff take him and carry him to the Common Whipping Post and give him thirty nine lashes on his bare back well laid on, also on the motion of JOHN Garzia, liberty is hereby given him to put an Iron Collar about his Legg with a wooden Clogg at the end of it to hinder him from running away (Sparacio. *Book 1721-1732* 566).

The leg clog did not prevent Mr. Warrell from again absenting himself from his master the following year. On November 6, 1732, the court ordered that he receive the standard punishment, for nine days absence and two hundred pounds of tobacco expended in the process of his procurement (Sparacio. *Book 1732-1739* 2).

Having a child out of wedlock was a criminal offence in colonial times and if the usual fine was not paid, the standard alternative punishment was whipping. The second indentured servant in the Garzia household, Elizabeth Parsons, was guilty of this crime, and the Reverend Garzia brought her to court on January fifth, 1731:

> PARSONS Whipt ELIZABETH PARSONS, Servant to Mr. JOHN GARZIA being brought to this Court by her Master for having a basterd Child and she refuseing to pay her fine it is therefore ordered that the Sheriff take her and carry her to the Common Whipping Post and give her twenty five lashes on her bare back well laid on (Sparacio. *Book 1721-1732* 613).

Parsons remained in the Reverend Garzia's employment as an indentured servant, but she was not satisfied with her situation. The next year on October 4, she was brought to trial "haveing fugitively absented herselfe from her Master's service for the space fifty seven days." (Sparacio. *Book 1721-1732* 657). She was returned to Parson Garzia's employment for only a few days when she again escaped, was recaptured, and underwent trial on November 7, 1732 for a fugitive absence of thirteen days (Sparacio *Book 1732-1739* 8). Parsons' trial was conducted just one day after the previously mentioned trial of her fellow servant, Mr. Warrell for his nine day absence, and Parsons was sentenced to the customary extensions of her indentured servitude for her two escapes.

Information concerning Thomas Warrell, Elizabeth Parsons, or any other servants of the Garzias in the Virginia or North Carolina records remains ambiguous. One is tempted to speculate regarding the origins and fates of these two individuals. One could wonder if they were willingly indentured, or if they were involuntarily indentured servants as a result of previous crimes. One could reasonably suspect that Warrell was the father of Parsons' child, and that his threatening of Mr. Garzia was prompted by Garzia's having reported the illegitimacy. It is possible that when the two servants escaped just weeks before the expected move to North Carolina, they went together and that they might have left in an attempt to avoid the Garzias' move to North Carolina. Perhaps they were attempting to escape further indentured service, since it would be very difficult to arrange their return to their master after his move to North Carolina. On the other hand, although there is no available evidence, it is also possible that these servants moved to North Carolina and completed their period of indentured service with the Garzias there.

During this period Parson Garzia himself was summoned to court by the grand jury in 1731 for allegedly exacting greater fees than the law allowed for marrying two couples. The charge was later dismissed (Sparacio. *Book 1729-32 583*, 592).

In addition to engaging in civil-type suits, Garzia was the victim of an assault. The Richmond County Grand Jury brought a bill of indictment against a Mr. William Dryas on May 3, 1732 for allegedly assaulting Garzia. The order is as follows:

> DRYAS to be summoned. Whereas the Grandjury for the body of this County having this day found a Bill of Indictment against WILLIAM DRYAS of Northfarnham Parish for making an assault upon the body of JOHN GARZIA, Clerk [cleric] of

51

the said Parish, it is therefore ordered that the Sheriff summon to the next Court the said WILLIAM DRYAS to answer the same (Sparacio. *Book 1721-1732* 646 and *Book 1732-1739* 97)

Unfortunately no record survives which explains Mr. Dryas's motive for attacking the parish priest. Eventually, after one continuation, the charges were dismissed, probably because, by then, Garzia had left the colony and was not present to testify.

Colonial North Carolina

Historian Hugh Lefler notes that the abundance of land and its ease of acquisition, the scarcity of capital, and the labor situation determined the economic and social order in colonial North Carolina. The chief forms of wealth were land and slaves; consequently the economic and social hierarchy of the colony was topped by planters. Class lines were sharply drawn. In the highest social stratum — along with the planters — were public officials and professional men, including members of the clergy (114). However, Garzia developed financial problems after his move to Bath, and though qualified as "upper class" by virtue of his profession, Garzia and his family may not have enjoyed the luxuries and prestige enjoyed by others in the gentry class.

Why John and Mary Garzia decided Bath Town, in the province of North Carolina, was preferable to Farnham in the province of Virginia and how they were persuaded to make the arduous move is another puzzle in the life of John Garzia. Farnham, which was a prosperous farming community at a crossroads location in Virginia's Northern Neck, offered many more cultural and material advantages than the much less-developed community of Bath. What is more, later history suggests that after the family's early period of financial instability, Garzia's compensation in Virginia was sufficient to accumulate some wealth — enough for him to arrive in North Carolina with considerable savings.

A possible contributing factor to Garzia's departure from Virginia may have been the dispute in his congregation concerning the location of a proposed new church. It had been decided that the church building where Garzia had officiated was so inadequate that it had to be abandoned (North Farnham Church Women 46).[1]

Perhaps Garzia genuinely believed that he was needed in North Carolina. Perhaps he was impressed by an attitude of dedication and sincerity in the St. Thomas Vestry in Bath. Whatever the reasons, after nine years in Virginia, the Garzias were persuaded to leave the community of John Garzia's first substantial ministry and the place where three of their children were born and two were buried.

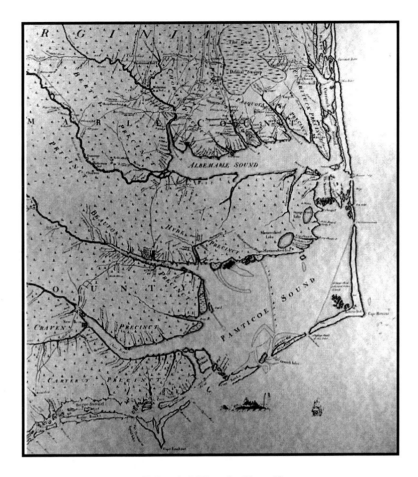

Colonial North Carolina

From A *New and Correct Map of the Province of North Carolina* by Moseley, 1733. On this map Bath Town is at the border of Hyde and Beaufort Precincts on Pamticoe River off of Pamticoe Sound. Through Permission of the Secial Collections Department, J.Y. Joyner Library, East Carolina University., Greenville, NC.

When the Garzia family first arrived in the colonies and most especially, in North Carolina, considerable adjustment was required. John and Mary Garzia had experienced the conveniences and comforts available in Dublin, the thriving cultural and commercial center of Ireland. However in North Carolina, except for a few plantation owners, life for the settlers was still "rough-hewn."

Resources in North Carolina were plentiful but money was scarce. Without doubt, the Garzias and their household, like their neighbors, either produced food, clothing, and household articles themselves or they bartered for these necessities. In addition to the fish, meat, and wild fruits and berries readily available in the woods and local waters, maize (Indian corn), tobacco, peas, beans, wheat, rice, apples, peaches, pears, plums, and figs were grown locally. Indian corn and pork were the mainstays for the ordinary family, but settlers also produced their own breads, beef, and dairy products, including butter and cheese. Surplus grains and fruits were processed into wine and whiskey, which colonial North Carolinians considered healthful. Cloth making from wool and flax was a major household chore and practically every home had its spinning wheel and loom. Except for the most wealthy plantation owners, homespun cloth and home-tanned cowhides and deerskins were used to produce clothing, shoes, harnesses, and other essentials. Local firewood was gathered for cooking and heating, and all but the most prosperous households molded their own candles, made their own soap, hauled their water and disposed of their waste. The Garzia household would have been a busy one.

Not withstanding the savings that he brought from Virginia, considering his financial situation, it is likely that the home that Garzia built in Bath, North Carolina, was rather modest. Except for the dwellings of a few wealthy settlers,[2] homes in colonial North Carolina in the early 1700s were plain and unpainted. They were customarily made of logs with mud caulking and wood shingle roofs. Houses most often consisted of one story with one or two rooms below and a ladder to a sleeping loft; sometimes there was a lean-to on the back. The interior was dark because there were few if any windows. Wooden floors were frequently absent in an ordinary home. Doors hung on wooden hinges. Locks were wooden and fastening was with wooden pegs. Chimneys of most homes were made from layered sticks and adobe. (Brick chimneys were a proud possession of the wealthy.) (Hawks 241). This modest type of home was most likely the Garzia dwelling.

  Overland travel by foot or horseback was difficult in "primitive" North Carolina. Roads were so poorly maintained and were so frequently interrupted by streams, sounds, and swamps as to be tediously slow, difficult, and, at times, dangerous. (See Moseley Map, p.55.) For heavy cargo, four-wheeled horse-drawn wagons could carry approximately 2000 pounds 40 miles a day and two-wheel carts could carry about half that much. Most of the plantations and farms and all of the important towns in colonial North Carolina's Coastal Plain were on or near navigable waterways that could handle ships carrying freight and passengers, and individual family units used canoes for their own local travel and fishing (Lefler 102-05). In the course of Parson Garzia's travels to visit parishioners, if he were fortunate, ferries were sometimes available for crossing rivers and sounds that threaded the area.

In addition to the difficulties of travel, the means of communication in North Carolina were slow, uncertain, and expensive. As early as 1715, a law was passed ordering that all "public dispatches" be carried promptly from plantation to plantation until they reached their destination, under penalty of £5 for each default (Lefler 112). Garzia's letters were sent by ship captains, traders, planters, or any other means that seemed convenient and modestly reliable.

Religion in Colonial North Carolina

A general understanding of the background of the religious history of the province of North Carolina prior to Garzia's arrival deepens a contemporary reader's understanding of the tasks that Garzia faced when he moved to the town of Bath.

As an early North Carolina historian Francis Hawks so aptly states: "It has long been a prevalent opinion that in the earliest portion of our history, the inhabitants of North Carolina lived in a state little short of downright heathenism. That there was a lamentable deficiency of piety and spiritual instruction is, indeed, but too true . . . [The settlers] were surrounded by dangers and troubles novel in character, and they wanted [lacked] both experience and means wherewith to overcome them. Uncertain of ultimate success, and worse still, uncertain of each other, they cohered not from religious sympathy, but rather, from the felt necessities and mutual dependence of their exiled condition" (335). In fact, there was yet no organized Church of England congregation in all of North Carolina by the end of the seventeenth century. The president of the Governor's Council,[1] Henderson Walker summed up the situation in 1703 when he wrote that "we have been settled neer 50 years in this place and I may justly say most part of 21 years on my owne knowledge without Priest or Alter and before that time according to that appears to me much worse" (Cain 22).

Before the eighteenth century, the only sustained religious activity in North Carolina, apart from Native American religious ceremonies, had been that of small congregations of the Society of Friends (Quakers) who were most active in the Perquimans and Pasquotank precincts in Albemarle County. Though North Carolina was noteworthy from its very beginnings for religious toleration, Quakers were not very numerous until a large Quaker population moved into Albermarle County after 1695 when John Archdale, a Quaker proprietor was appointed Governor of Carolina (an area today comprising both North and South Carolina). Francis Hawks describes the Friends' migration into North Carolina: "Persecution sent them into the wilderness of North Carolina, and this persecution began in New England . . . and after being deprived of all their goods, to be banished from Virginia? And if such treatment drove Quakers, as it did, into the wilderness of North Carolina, where (God be thanked) they were permitted to stay in peace, unpersecuted and unwhipped, — we ask, which best deserved to be called a harbor for rogues, the place to which they fled, or that from which they came?" (361).

    The Quakers held the balance of power in the province in the late sixteen hundreds, and under Governor Archdale, Quakers controlled the colonial government. Anglicans were determined to regain control through regulations "establishing" the Church of England. They were aided in this endeavor by two developments. One was the appointment in 1699 of Henderson Walker, a zealous member of the Church of England, as governor; the second was, at the urging of Governor Walker, the sending of missionaries from London (Cain xxiv, 14n). The Bishop of London, Dr. Henry Compton, appointed Dr. Thomas Bray to be Compton's commissary in Maryland in 1695. Bray's report when he returned to London, five years later, stated the need for missionaries and for libraries to be provided to these missionaries (Hawks 338). Bray also proposed a method to raise funds for the support of this enterprise. He suggested that all bishops in the mother country contribute annually and that they use their influence to persuade others in their diocese to do the same. In his report he spoke of North Carolina.

> Roanoak [Albermarle settlement] lyes betwixt Virginia and Carolina. It is peopled with English, intermixt with the native Indians to a great extent; and as there will be occasion for at least two missionaries to be sent among them, so the governor, who is now going over to that colony, being a very worthy gentleman, I dare promise will give the best countenance and encouragement which shall be in his power. The last province that I shall now speak of on the continent is Carolina [In the lords proprietor's patent all the territory south of Albermarle] a very thriving colony, and so large as to want at least three missionaries, beside one lately sent thither (Hawks 339).

Prompted by Dr. Bray's report, Dr. Compton went to the king and obtained a bounty of £20 for every minis-

61

ter or schoolmaster who would remove to America. Unfortunately, the Carolinas profited little by this bounty because only comparatively rich settlements could afford to support a priest after he arrived.

Dr. Bray worked diligently to promote a mission field for Anglicanism in the colonies. In 1699 he formed the Society for the Promotion of Christian Knowledge (SPCK). This organization concentrated its efforts on establishment of schools and libraries and on the printing of doctrinal literature (Cain xxxix).

In 1701, another society was formed, again through the efforts of Thomas Bray. This society was chartered by King William III for the purpose of supplying the American colonies with clergymen. It was named the "Society for the Propagation of the Gospel in Foreign Parts" (SPG) and is the oldest existing Protestant missionary association in the world (Hawks 340). To this organization, chiefly, the Protestant Episcopal Church in North America may be said to owe its existence.

In 1700, through the efforts of Dr. Bray and the Society for the Promotion of Christian Knowledge, the Reverend Daniel Brett was sent to Albermarle County, North Carolina, even before the SPG had commenced its activities. Brett brought with him a library that was donated by Thomas Thynne, First Viscount of Weymouth, and delivered the library to St. Thomas Parish in 1701. This library contained materials of three types: the provincial materials were intended for use by the whole province, the parochial materials were for the use of the incumbent priest, and the "laymen's library" was for the use of the laity of the parish. This collection of books comprised the first public library in North Carolina, and it remained as an object of much civic pride in Bath for many years. However, by 1760 all the volumes had been dispersed, and the library as such no longer exists, except for a single volume, Gabriel Towerson's <u>An Explication to the Catechism of the Church of England</u>, London, 1685, which is a prized possession of present day St. Thomas Church in Bath (Cain xli-xlii).

Evidently Dr. Bray had been deceived in his opinion of the character of Mr. Brett. After Brett had been in residence in North Carolina for about six months, Governor Walker complained to the Bishop of London that "it hath been a great trouble and grief to us who have a great veneration for the Church that the first minister who was sent us should prove so ill as to give the Dissenters so much occasion to charge us with him" (Lefler 59). Mr. Brett's disgraceful behavior caused him to leave the colony of North Carolina around January 1703. The precise nature of his offenses was never stated by Brett's detractors, but their characterization of him as "Scandalous Beast," "the Monster of the Age," "the worst . . . that ever came over" indicate that they must have been serious (Cain 15, 22, 74, 498).

Though Brett was a bad beginning, the presence of this unworthy minister in the colony was indirectly beneficial. His presence caused the laity to realize the need to build churches and to provide for the maintenance of clergy. Despite Quaker opposition, Walker and the proponents of "establishment" passed the "Vestry Act" of 1701— the first church law in North Carolina. It provided for the official establishment of the Church of England and for the laying out of parishes. It also addressed the organization of vestries, the building of churches, and the collection of a poll tax on all "tithables" in order to support the established church and its clergymen. The Vestry

Act was then referred to the Lords Proprietors for their verification. In the meantime, about 1702, even before the Vestry Act was approved by the Proprietors, the first Episcopal church was built in North Carolina somewhere around the present town of Edenton. A year later Governor Walker recorded that two more church buildings were being erected by vestries in the Albermarle region (Hawks 341).

However, the 1701 Vestry Act did not meet with universal approval. The Quakers, the small group of Presbyterians, and even some Anglicans objected to the act — some on religious principles and some because it increased taxes. This diverse group of objectors was determined to repeal the act at the next session of the colonial Assembly, one in which there was expected to be a Quaker majority — but this was not to be. The question was never considered in the assembly because, in London, the Proprietors finally rejected the law in 1703 on the grounds that it gave too much authority to individual parish vestries and that it did not provide adequate salaries for clergy.

Quaker celebration was, however, short-lived. The newly installed governor, Robert Daniel, was even more active for the official establishment of Anglicanism than Walker had been. In the year 1704 he wrote the SPG that when news of a modification of the Oath of Abjuration which had been enacted by the new monarch, Queen Anne, reached North Carolina "the Quakers refuseing to take, they were dissmissd [from] the Council, Assembly and Courts of Justice and a Law made that none Should bear any Office or Place of Trust without takeing the Said Oaths" (Cain 82). The requirement that they take an oath denied the "right of affirmation," to which the Quakers had been entitled for years.[2] The law was also so resented by the Presbyterians, that they joined the Quakers in removing Daniel from office in 1705[3] (Lefler 60).

Into this extremely unstable setting at the start of the eighteenth century, the SPG sent the Reverend Mr. John Blair, North Carolina's first missionary. Lord Weymouth (Thomas Thynne), who deplored the poor religious state of the colonists, contributed £50 toward the support of Mr. Blair who had also received the queen's bounty of £20. Hawks reports that Blair "landed in Virginia on the 14th of January 1703/4. On the 24th, he was at his work in Albermarle, with the goodness of the Lord and His power, as his best stock; and £25 in his pocket to live on, while he endeavored to evangelize a community which, with some few exceptions, was probably as near heathenism as any community calling itself Christian ever was" (Hawks 342). Mr. Blair found it necessary to hire a guide and to supply himself and his guide with horses. This one man was entrusted to see to the spiritual needs not only of those in the Albermarle region but also the spiritual needs of the settlers on the Pamlico — people who could be reached only by a journey of fifty miles through a wilderness occupied by "savages." Within two months this dedicated man was forced to support himself by disposing of his personal belongings. He found the three churches that had been built, one in each of the precincts of Chowan, Perquimans, and Pasquotank. In each he assigned readers who were to read Morning and Evening Prayer on each Sunday that he was not present. They were to read, also, two sermons from books in the library that the SPG had furnished him. He convened vestries in each precinct and the good man naively relayed a proposal from Dr. Bray that, if the vestries would provide glebes for each church, there would likely be attached to each glebe, "such as there is in the Island of Bromudas, two slaves and a small stock." This plan would provide a perpetual income for incumbent priests (Cain 28). The hardworking Blair traveled, on average, 30 miles a day, except for Sundays when he preached twice and traveled still further, and he often slept in the woods when night approached (Hawks 342-44). In all, Blair baptized about 100 persons but he avoided performing marriage ceremonies because that would have deprived the magistrates of their fees for this service. Though his circumstances were desperate, Blair persevered in his work with the expectation that the Assembly, when it met, would make provisions for his support. Unfortunately, the Vestry Act of 1701 had come back from the Proprietors disapproved. (Ironically, it was rejected because the proprietors deemed the proposed ministerial stipend of £30 as too *little*.) To make matters worse, the Assembly was now dominated by Quakers, who were not, in any case, inclined to reenact the Vestry Law and its salary increase for Anglican clergy (Cain 27-30). Circumstances went from bad to worse for Mr. Blair who was penniless and had no place to turn. Finally, some of his friends and supporters furnished their priest with funds and advised him to return to England immediately. He took their advice, but his ship was captured by the French, and he was detained in France for nine weeks as a prisoner of war. Blair finally reached England in November 1704. He was destitute and had accrued a huge debt. The poor man reported to the Society that "although I was sent to the most Barbarous place in the continent, yet I had no more than my £50 per annum from my Ld. Weymouth, for I never Could have Expected to have got a Farthing from the Country had I stayed there

7 years longer" (Cain 31). Thus ends the story of the first Anglican missionary to North Carolina.

The Society, to its credit, took the report of Mr. Blair into account when it renewed its efforts to plant the Church of England in North Carolina. Though there were not funds to send four missionaries (as he recommended), the SPG did send two; and further, the Society made better provisions for their support. In 1708 these ministers, Mr. James Adams and Mr. William Gordon, reached Virginia after three months' sailing. They then traveled in a sloop to Albermarle County, and by common agreement, Mr. Gordon took charge of the precincts of Chowan and Perquimans and Mr. Adams took charge of the precincts of Pasquotank and Currituck (Hawks 345).

The Reverends Mr. Adams and Mr. Gordon served admirably, notwithstanding the efforts of the Quakers to interfere with the Anglicans' work. The two traveled faithfully throughout the four precincts, preaching and baptizing and administering the Eucharist wherever they could gather a congregation (Hawks 345-50).

North Carolina would undoubtedly have continued to benefit from the ministries of Adams and Gordon, but for the advent of the worst period in the civic life of the early colony. Beginning in 1708 two factions contended for the leadership of the colony. One was headed by Thomas Cary who, to regain his leadership, had allied himself with the Quakers who were contesting provisions of the Vestry Act. The other faction was led by William Glover, who as President of the Council, had assumed leadership when Governor Cary was in South Carolina and then refused to relinquish power when Cary returned. The result was lawlessness and confusion for two years. Eventually the Proprietors, who were not pleased with the resulting governmental chaos, sent Edward Hyde to assume the position of colonial governor and to restore order. Cary reacted with armed force in the year 1711, but was captured, and the "Cary Rebellion" ended with Cary's being transported to England for trial (Lefler 60-61). This conflict, coupled with an epidemic of yellow fever and a series of bad crop years, left the colony in a very weak and demoralized state. Revengeful Indians saw an opportunity to attack, and the massacre of September 22, 1711, marked the beginning of the Tuscarora Wars. Small native bands attacked colonial settlements from the Neusiok (Neuse) to the Pamlico — killing, scalping, and burning. Colonists fortunate enough to escape fled to Bath or to fortified homes, and Bath itself was reduced from 16 to 13 homes during the conflict[4] (Lefler 64).

Early in this period of governmental turmoil and religious dissension, the Rev. Mr. Gordon became so discouraged that he gave up on his ministry in North Carolina and returned to England. His departure was a great disappointment to many people of the Albermarle, but especially to his friend and confidant, Mr. Adams. Mr. Adams continued his work until a year later when, physically worn out by the hardships he had endured, he decided that he also must leave North Carolina. He wrote the Society in London that:

> I have lived here in a dismal Countrey about two Years and a half where I have suffer'd a World of misery and trouble both in body and mind. I have gone through good report and evil report, and endured as much I think as any of Your Missionarys has done before me, wherefore I humbly pray and hope the Honorable

> Society will now be pleased to Alter my Mission to South Carolina where I doubt not but by God's Assistance, I shall be able to do more good, and whoever succeeds me here will have this Advantage that none of the Countrey will be prejudiced to his Person (as all who adhered to the Quakers are to mine) and this in my Opinion will not conduce a little to the Success of his Labors (Cain 107).

It was resolved that Mr. Adams was to return to England, but he was literally worn out, and just when he was ready to embark, he became sick and died in Currituck in October 30, 1710. As a result, North Carolina again was without any Anglican clergy.

The next clergyman sent by the SPG was the Reverend Mr. John Urmstone (variously spelled) who, in 1710, settled in Chowan with his wife, three children, and two servants. Hawks presents an unflattering sketch of Urmstone and the cleric's eleven year ministry in North Carolina:

> Born in Lancashire, he had received a university education, and, we are constrained to believe, had taken orders, as too many in the Church of England did in that day rather as a means of support than from any deep sense of duty to God. Unamiable in disposition and ready to quarrel, he was covetous also, and very much disposed to presume on the dignity of his sacred office. The most querimonious of men, every letter is filled with complaints of his unparalleled sufferings, and solemn assurances of

the impending starvation of himself and his family; while they generally wind up with a pathetic farewell to his English friends, and a business-like announcement that he had drawn certain bills of exchange which he wished duly honored, not forgetting to add instructions as to the remittances in English goods, which he assures his saddened countrymen he can sell at an excellent profit. Six times in ten years he assured them that he expected himself and family to be laid in the tomb from sheer *want of food,* before he could possibly hear from England; and yet he orders a variety of articles to be sent, which could not possibly arrive until, upon his hypothesis, the grave would have hidden alike him and his necessities. And yet this man, thus eternally starving, contrived to buy land and negroes and stock, to hire white servants, to procure tools and agricultural implements, to be the proprietor of horses and boats; and, in short, appears to have been the only missionary, during the proprietary rule, that ever acquired any property in the country; while from his letters we gather the fact, that he administered the Lord's Supper but *twice in five years!* More acrimonious bitterness of speech than he uses concerning those whom he disliked, it would be difficult to find; and the significant fact presents itself, that those whom he most reviles were really the most seriously religious of the Churchmen in the province. The coarseness of his language harmonizes with the malignity of his temper; it as little became the refinement of a gentleman as it did the holiness of a priest: thus the province is designated a "hell of a hole;" and he declares that he would rather be "the curate of Bear Garden than bishop of Carolina." He was perpetually quarrelling with his vestries, and always about money; and, in a word, succeeded to admiration [admirably] in very speedily making himself odious and unpopular among people of all classes, by his impiety and selfishness . . . The very records of the court show him to have been punished for *drunkenness and profanity* and the enemies of Christianity could not have desired a more efficient auxiliary than the presence in the province of such a man as the Rev. John Urmstone (Hawks 351-52).

In 1716 the Society agreed with Mr. Urmstone's request to return to England, but he did not receive the letter authorizing his return until 1720, and he left only after he had settled his affairs to his advantage in 1721. Mr. Urmstone then served "tempestuous" missions in the Middle Atlantic region, and finally died in a fire in Maryland (Cain 502).

During the early years of Urmstone's pastorate, another missionary of the Society, the Reverend Giles Rainsford arrived in North Carolina in May 1712. He settled on the west side of the Chowan, whereas Urmstone was on the east side of the river. Hawks writes that Urmstone and Rainsford soon developed a hearty dislike for one another and, in letters to the Society, each accused the other of malingering and various other failings. Mr. Rainsford was not very energetic in his efforts to adjust to the challenges of the situation or to spread the gospel. Perhaps this was due to timidity and preoccupation with other matters. He ran up considerable debt through bills of exchange, and much of his correspondence to the Society concerned his expectation that the Society would pay his obligations (Cain 501-2). At one time he was captured and detained by Indians, and finally, after a few months he became so alarmed by Indian hostilities that he withdrew into Virginia (Hawks 353).[5] Rainsford made a few more relatively short visits into North Carolina, but he eventually secured a parish in Virginia through the influence of its governor. Rainsford resigned as a SPG missionary in 1714, furious at having several of his bills of exchange refused by the Society (Cain 502).

In the interval between the arrivals of the Reverends Urmstone and Rainsford, North Carolina's new governor, Charles Eden — who was a St. Thomas Parish vestryman in Bath County — appealed to the SPG to assign the Reverend Mr. Thomas Gale[6] to Bath County (See Appendix C for the full text of Eden's letter). In his letter to the SPG, the governor pointed out the deplorable state of religion in the province and the desperate need for clergymen. He stated that Mr. Urmstone "is not able to Serve one half of the county of Albermarle which Adjoins to Virginia, when the county of Bath of a much larger extant is wholly destitute of any Assistance." Eden further stated that "our Tedious Indian Warr has reduced the Country so lowe" that without help from the SPG, those settlers who had retained any "resemblance of it [religion] would be led away by the Quakers, whereas a few of the Clergy of a Complaisant temper and Regular lives would not only be the darlings of the people but would be a means in time to recover those already Seduced by Quakerism" (Cain 186). Evidently Thomas Gale was not aware that he was being recommended to the SPG by Governor Eden for an assignment to Bath County in North Carolina, and in fact, did not want to move there as his letter of August 1715 states:

> Honored Sir
> By letters from my eldest Brother Major Christopr Gale of Bath-Town in No. Carolina, I find myself recommended to the Honorable society for propagation of the Gos- pel in Forreign parts, to be sent as a Missionary into No. Carolina, and therein to the county of Bath, which at present is without any Clergy-man, and stands in great need (as my Brother's letters both to my Father the Rector of Kighley, and me Minister of Carlton nigh snathe do set forth). Now I do heartily wish the promotion of the Gospel in the Country and had I been single, should not have excus'd myself, but as the case stands, being married into a family that will by no means hear of my leaving this country, I crave leave to be excused, wishing some one more worthy than myself mayh undertake that work heartily, and perform it faithfully. I

pray my humble service may be given to the Honorable Society from
(Sir) yr. Very Humble Servant
[Addressed]
To the Secretary of the Honorable
Society for propagation of the Gospel in Forreign Parts
[Endorsed]
Mr. Thomas Gale (Cain 204).

The Society, after consideration of these letters then "Agreed that Mr. Commissary[7] (Gideon) Johnston (in South Carolina) with the Advice and Approbation of the rest of the Clergy do Appoint one of their Number a Single man and one who has been obliged to leave his Parish, to repair to North Carolina and officiate as the Society's Missionary there and that a Letter be wrote to him accordingly." The gentleman in South Carolina that the Society had in mind for this move to Bath County was the Reverend Ebenezer Taylor because it was well known that South Carolina was trying to get rid of him. Johnston's response to the Society revealed that he had requested the "Advise and Approbation of the rest of the (South Carolina) Clergy" and he reported that "and upon a Short Debate the Choice fell upon Mr. Taylor unanimously" (Cain 206-08). It is doubtful that there was much debate. In fact there must have been jubilation. Mr. Taylor was despised by his fellow clergy as well as well as by parishioners. In a letter to the Society, the Reverend Johnston declared:

> The plain truth on't is (for I dare not conceal a thing of this Importance from my most Honoured Superiours) we are all of Opinion that he would do better elsewere

than here; neither his peevish and uneasie Temper or his self conceit and Obstinious or his Way of Preaching which is alltogether upon the Old Presbyterian Way, or his too penurious and covetous Rate of Life, being at all agreeable to his Brethren, his Parishioners, or indeed to any one in the whole country (Cain 206).

Mr. Johnston was justified in including Taylor's flock among those who were unhappy with the man. In a letter to Mr. Johnston in October 1716, the parishioners of St. Andrews made their dislike of Mr. Taylor clear and listed their reasons "why Mr. Ebenezr. Taylor should be no Longer Suffered to officiate in the said Parish." Among the listed complaints were: "1st. His uncharitable railing in his Sermons, Taxing his Parishioners, and the whole Province with the most Heinous and gross Crimes that can be invented . . . 3dly. Not Administering the Holy Sacrament on Christmas Day, or so much as reading the proper or any other Psalms on that Day . . . 6thly. Not keeping to the Prayers of the church but entering into a long and unmannerly Exposition with God Almighty, after the Method of the meanest and most ignorant of the Presbyterians . . . 7thly. Neglecting to pray for the Sick when desired . . . 8thly. Being so sordidly Covetous that he is an Offence to Modesty, not allowing himself Britches or Stockings; And endeavouring to Stop Part of his poor Clerks Salary, because himself sat the Psalm sometimes when the Clerk was impress'd and at the Camp, [on military duty] and quarreling with Several Vestrys, for refuseing to pay him for two Sermons he preach'd 'ere he was elected, even to that Degree that no Business can be done, by Means whereof the Church is greatly out of Repair and hitherto intirely Neglected . . . 10thly. In allmost all his Sermons presumeing to add even to God Almighty's own Words, and Composeing his Discourses of Non-Sensicall Repetitions . . . 11thly. Quarrelling with and abuseing his Parishioners calling them gross Names: As Mr. Miles whom he called Old Rogue and Old Villain. And upon the said Miles his answering that if he was so he desired to be instructed otherwise by him, the said Taylor returned, in a great Passion you are past it you are past it" (Cain 228-30).

    Mr. Taylor himself made it clear that he also was not pleased with the proposed transfer to Bath County, North Carolina. Commissary Johnston wrote the Secretary of the SPG in April 1716 that:

> Sir...
>
> Mr. Taylor continues still the Same Unhappy Man, And has added that of a Notorious and common Reviler and Slanderer of all his Parishioners and Brethren, to the rest of his good Qualities; And has been so Spitefull and Malicious as not to converse with some of his Parish or ever be in the Same Company with them at my House; tho' it was his undoubted Interest to compose and settle Things by all the mild and Christian Methods he could. He uses me very Scurvily; and threatens me as he does all the Rest of Mankind, but this, I thank God gives me not the least uneasyness.
>
> I am, Sir, Your most humble Servant.
>   Gideon Johnston. (Cain 216).

    The Secretary also received a very long letter from Mr. Taylor:

> Sir, Thus have I been fighting With Saint Paul's Beasts at Ephesus, and casting my Pearls before Swine for near 4 Years and they have been trampling them under their Feet and turning again upon me, and renting me all this While, and the Fight is not yet over but it is so far from this, that the Battle is now hotte then ever against me, for now my Enemies have got Mr. Commissary on their Side, and he assists them mightily, and now I must unavoidably be Vanquisht and devoured, if the Society, and my Lord of London do not defend and preserve me, as I hope they will.

Mr. Taylor continued that he was a married man, and it had been recommended that the Society send a single man. He then suggested, by name, two single missionaries who in his view would be better candidates for North Carolina than he. He further informed the Society that

> I can't think, because they really judg'd me the most proper Person, for my Age and the Pains I have been this long Time and am Still continually under and above all being so very much Inferiour to all my Brethren in Parts and Abillityes, as I understand they themselves think me and as I readily acknowledg my self to be, make me the most improper person of them all for this Mission (Cain 217-220).

Finally however, Mr. Taylor realized he must go to North Carolina or lose the financial support of the Society. He had been ordered to Bath County, but

Fearing it would be a much longer time before I should meet with a Passage directly to North Carolina (which indeed would have been the most convenient for me because of My Sores, which rendered me alltogether unfit for Travail by Land either on Foot or on Horseback) I embrac'd a Passage for Hampton River in Virginia where we arriv'd the 8th of July following, and where I was forced to stay till the 5th of September . . . I met with a passage by Water there in one of those Sloops, where we Arriv'd the Ninth following and on the,25th following I got to the South west Shore of Chowan" (Cain 258-262).

Because his sores interfered with land travel, Mr. Taylor decided to stay on the Chowan shore rather than move on to his assignment in Bath County. He experienced little public interest in his ministry there, so after a year, he moved to Perquimans Precinct, where he experienced even less support. By November 1719, he was in Bath Town where he had been invited by the governor and the vestry of St. Thomas Parish. He found no better reception in Bath and shortly packed his belongings in his own boat with his own crew and headed for a settlement in Core Sound, the southernmost settlement in the province. Unfortunately he was careless enough to permit his crew to discover that he had with him a considerable sum of money. On their way, they landed on Harbor Island at the mouth of the Neuse, but Mr. Taylor never left the island alive. According to a letter from Urmstone to the Society:

> There were some people on the island hunting for hoggs that had been placed there, who with those that went with him buried him and then rifled his Chests and divided the Spoile and are not to be brought to any Acct. Some of them have been purged by Oaths but that is of little force with a North Carolina Man (Cain 269).

The story related by the crew was that Taylor, having been tossed about in an open boat for ten days, died of the cold in February 1720. None of the crew perished, however, and the authorities suspected that Taylor was murdered. Officials in Edenton instituted inquiries but never determined his fate or recovered his money. One of the crew was prosecuted for "Felloniously taking Some money belonging to Eben-Ezer Taylor" but the sailor escaped from jail and fled the colony (Cain 270).

With Mr. Taylor's death, the only Anglican priest remaining in North Carolina was Mr. Urmstone, the man who had claimed to the SPG a decade previously that he had only a short time left to live because he was being starved. He departed from North Carolina, apparently healthy, in 1721. Upon his departure, except for the Society of Friends, the province was left without any organized religion at all.

Governor Eden again appealed to the Society that some clergy be sent and accordingly Mr. Thomas Newman settled in the Southwest Parish of Chowan with his "little family" in 1722. He energetically served Southwest Parish and Society Parish in Bertie Precinct. He traveled far and wide preaching and baptizing in the remotest parts of the province. On one trip to Bath, he baptized hundreds of children, but the natural consequences of his exposure and unremitting toil were frequent illness and finally death after less than two years in North Carolina, a great loss to the region. He had so endeared himself to the community that the Assembly, after his death, voted £40 to his widow to assist her in her passage home. The SPG also expressed its appreciation by presenting her his whole year's salary of £60 (Cain 501).

Considering the foregoing accounts, it is not surprising that North Carolina had become an unpopular option for English clergymen who sought positions as missionaries in the colonies. Few were willing to undergo the hardships and risks involved in ministering to such an unpromising province. So North Carolina was again without Anglican clergy.

It was not until the next year, April 1725, when Sir Richard Everard was made governor, that another missionary was assigned to the province of North Carolina. At the request of the Lords Proprietors, the Reverend Mr. John Blacknall was appointed by the SPG. He accompanied the new governor from England and was received as a minister in the town of Edenton. Little is known of Mr. Blacknall's ministry in North Carolina. Evidently he became involved in a political dispute between his patron Governor Everard and the former governor, George Burrington, and by July 1726 had moved to Virginia where he remained for the rest of his life (Cain 497-8). There is, however, a remarkable entry in the court records of Chowan precinct concerning Blacknall. By law, whites could marry only whites, and in the case of intermarriage, there was a stiff penalty imposed on the parties marrying and the clergyman or magistrate who performed the ceremony. Both the couple and the officiant were fined

£50. One half of the fines then was awarded to the informant and one half to the government. The record reveals that Mr. Blacknall informed "against _____, of Curratuck precinct, for joining himself in marriage to _____, a mulatto woman." Surprisingly, Blacknall was the one who performed the ceremony. He evidently was the perpetrator who paid a £50 fine and the informant who received a total of £50 reward, breaking even on the "transaction" (Hawks 126).

Before Mr. Blacknall had left Carolina, another clergyman, the Reverend Thomas Baylye (also spelled Baily) appeared. Since he was not a missionary of the Society, he was not directly supported by that organization. Around 1717, Mr. Baylye had resigned from a parish in Maryland following complaints about his drunkenness, swearing and quarrelling. In 1721, Governor Spotswood of Virginia reported that Baylye had "thrust himself" into a living in two parishes without the Virginia governor's having given him permission. Commissary James Blair of Virginia later wrote that Mr. Baylye had scandalized the colony by his drunkenness and fighting. When he was no longer tolerated in Virginia, Baylye moved to North Carolina and began officiating in Pasquotank and Perquimans precincts in 1725. He soon became a supporter of former governor George Burrington in Burrington's conflict with Governor Richard Everard. Everard wrote to the Bishop of London that following two days of drunkenness after Baylye's arrival in Edenton, Baylye asked permission to preach. Everard refused and Baylye, at the urging of Burrington, broke down the court house door and conducted a religious service in the courthouse (Hawks 355-56). Immediately thereafter, Mr. Baylye left Edenton and went to Bath where he presumably ministered to the in-

81

habitants there and in Hyde precinct until his return to England in 1729. (Commissary Blair had given Baylye the funds necessary to return to England, since no congregation in North Carolina, Virginia, or Maryland would any longer tolerate Baylye.) Shortly after Baylye's arrival in England, he solicited funds from the SPG and presented a forged petition from the vestries of Hyde precinct and St. Thomas Parish, Bath, extolling his services to them. Though he was never in its service, the Society gave him £10 (Cain 497). But back in North Carolina there was not, again, a single establishment clergyman.

The next clergyman to officiate in North Carolina was the Reverend Mr. John LaPierre who arrived in 1728, the last year of government by the Lords Proprietors. This devoted priest had served as a missionary of the SPG in South Carolina for twenty years prior to his move to North Carolina. Mr. LaPierre was the first Anglican minister to settle in the lower Cape Fear region, but he soon experienced competition from another more flamboyant priest, the Rev. Mr. Richard Marsden. An insufficient maintenance due to Marsden's competition led Mr. LaPierre to move to New Bern in Craven Parish in 1735. Though he was never installed as rector at Christ Church, LaPierre was active in conducting services and establishing congregations until his death in 1755 (Cain 500).

The colorful Reverend Mr. Richard Marsden arrived in the new Cape Fear settlement in 1729, just a year after the arrival of Mr. LaPierre. Marsden was one of the most controversial clerics to serve in colonial North Carolina. His ministry and commercial dealings involved many locations, and his travel was extensive. He was a cleric in Maryland, South Carolina, England, Barbados, Pennsylvania, Jamaica, New England, and Virginia before his move to North Carolina. In 1729 Marsden appeared in the Cape Fear settlement claiming falsely to be an itinerant missionary and an inspector of clergy. After making a commercial trip to Portugal, he returned to the Cape Fear where he made himself a popular figure, soon encroaching upon the position of Mr. LaPierre. In 1738 the SPG tentatively appointed Marsden missionary to the region, but the Bishop of London objected and the appointment was withdrawn. Marsden's attempts at reinstatement over the next few years were unsuccessful, and his clerical career was ended. A minister who knew Marsden while he was in South Carolina was of the opinion that Marsden's "itching for trading which he does not understand has been the cause of his misfortunes." Among these "misfortunes" were his having drawn fraudulent bills of exchange, escaping to flee prosecution for debt, and imprisonment for defrauding some trusting merchants of their cargo. Cain states that commercial misdeeds were not Marsden's only failings. While living in Jamaica, Marsden contracted a bigamous marriage with a wealthy widow, but, despite his failings, this persuasive cleric was able to convince many of his worthiness: he was in fact complimented in their writings by influential Virginians William Byrd and Commissary James Blair (500-01).

The religious history of colonial North Carolina would not be complete without mention of the Reverend Mr. Bevil Granville who, though he was only present in the colony for one year, had an admirable affect on the region's religious development. He was passing through North Carolina in 1732 en route from Dublin to Maryland and to a clerical position which was being sponsored by Lord Baltimore. Christopher Gale, the former Chief Justice who now lived in the Chowan precinct, and Governor

George Burrington prevailed on Granville to remain in North Carolina. Private donations were raised, and the vestry of St. Paul's parish (Edenton) paid his salary to officiate there and in the surrounding area for one year. In a letter to Bishop Gibson of London, Granville wrote that he was willing to stay in North Carolina because the need for clergy was so great, a need demonstrated by the fact that he had baptized nearly a thousand persons in his brief tenure in North Carolina. But by April 1733 Granville had moved on to Maryland (Cain 335, 341, 499).

Religious historian Robert Cain writes that during the same period (in 1732) the SPG assigned the newly ordained Reverend Mr. John Boyd to serve as an itinerant missionary in the province of North Carolina. Prior to going to London for ordination, Boyd had practiced medicine in Virginia for seven years. There he had developed a "scandalous reputation" which may be the cause of his having left that province; however, he was ordained in London, reputation notwithstanding.

Boyd was expected to officiate as an itinerant missionary in every part of the province of North Carolina — which was, of course, impossible.[8] He worked in Bertie Precinct until around 1735 when the SPG instructed him to move to Edenton. The scandalous behaviors of Boyd when he was in Virginia appear in no way to have abated when he served as an Anglican missionary in North Carolina. Governor Gabriel Johnston and other officials complained that Mr. Boyd was a drunkard and that he neglected his duties. In 1738 the SPG divided the North Carolina mission field into two parts, and despite the complaints about him, Boyd was assigned the part north and east of the Neuse. However, he never served in that capacity. He died in May 1738 (Cain 498).

Bath Town

Settlement in the Pamtico (alternatively Pamptico; the modern spelling is Pamlico) River region of North Carolina started around 1690 when French Huguenot refugees migrated from the James River area of Virginia. About eight years later, inhabitants of the Albermarle region in northeastern North Carolina began moving south and started farming on the banks of rivers and creeks of the Pamlico (Hawks 84). In order to encourage more settlement in their holdings, the Lords Proprietors instructed Governor John Archdale to designate more counties "for ye better regulating and ye encouragement of ye people." Accordingly, in 1696, Bath County was created (Lefler 54). This new district included the territory between the Albermarle Sound and Cape Fear River. Bath County would eventually compromise four precincts: Beaufort, Hyde, Craven, and Carteret. Beaufort Precinct, which encompassed the Pamlico River and its branches, formed a parish which was named "St. Thomas."

By the time John Garzia began his ministry in St. Thomas Parish, many noteworthy events had occurred in Bath County in the 37 years since its creation. John Lawson had ended his historic inland trip there in 1701. Lawson had laid out the town of Bath, and in 1705/06, Bath was incorporated as the first town in the colony of North Carolina. Unfortunately Lawson did not live long enough to see the new town prosper. Tuscarora Indians captured and executed him in 1711, and many settlers in Bath County were massacred in the Tuscarora Wars that started later that same year. A year later (in 1712) Christopher Gale, a Bath Town resident, and owner of the plantation Kirby Grange was appointed first Chief Justice of North Carolina.

Though Bath grew very slowly, it was a center of political and commercial importance for a few years after its incorporation, and the town was designated the first official port of entry in North Carolina in the year 1715. Three years later piracy along the Coast had reached its climax and Blackbeard (Edward Teach), whose home port was Bath, was killed near Ocracoke Inlet (Lefler 718).

Though Bath Town was politically and commercially important to the region during the early eighteenth century, it failed to develop. Just fifteen years after the port of entry was established, Governor George Burrington described Bath as "a town where [only] little improvements have been made" (Lefler 68).

None of the early missionaries sent by the SPG made much of an attempt to serve Bath County. Most of the residents in this hard-to-reach and sparsely populated frontier region were scattered along the shores of the Pamlico, and for missionaries to reach many of the settlers would have been both difficult and time consuming. Clergy as wandering adventurers from the West Indies and from other colonies had paid brief visits to Bath Town, but none had stayed long.

In spite of the difficulties and to their great credit, some of the earliest settlers in St. Thomas Parish longed to have a minister who would faithfully minister to their needs, and they were persistent in their efforts to attract one. Though they were without benefit of either a church or clergy, they had laid out a glebe[1] and conducted church services. It is recorded that Kirby Grange, the plantation of Christopher Gale, was used as a place of worship for Gale's family and neighbors (Hawks 360), and it is likely that books from the library donated by Dr. Bray were used by appointed readers in those services.

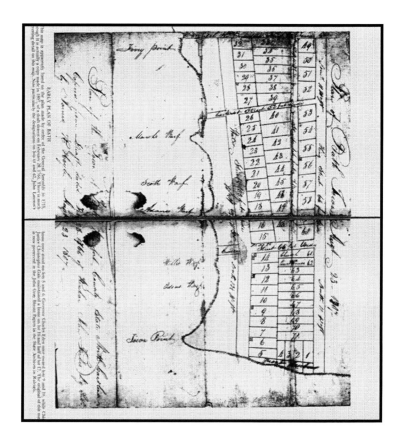

Early Plan of Bath Town

This map is based on the plan made in 1715. Note the designation of lots 61 and 62 for "Church" and "Court House." John Lawson's home stood on lots 5 and 6. Governor Eden owned lots 9 and 10 and Christopher Gale had a home on lot 16 and part of 17. John Garzia's home-site was on lots 49, 50 and 51. From the John Grey Blount Papers, Courtesy of the North Carolina Office of Archives and History, Raleigh, NC.

In 1717 the Church wardens and Vestry of St. Thomas Parish appealed to the SPG in a letter (See Appendix D) which Christopher Gale personally delivered along with his own appeal to the SPG. In their letter the Churchwardens and Vestry stated that, encouraged by the successes of the Society, they "[h]umbly recommend our present circumstances with that of the Neighboring Parishes in Bath county to Yr. pious care and consideration and to Implore Yr. Further Assistance." The writers of the letter pointed out that the SPG had assigned several missionaries to their parish (St. Thomas) and adjacent parishes, but that "as yet wee have not been so happy to have one Missionary resident in all the country" and that of all the missionaries who had come to the colony "it had been very rare that they have So much as Vizited these parts." The writers pledged themselves to maintain the customary per annum missionary salary "although at present there are a few of the parishes where the five Shillings per pole will not fully amount to the £50.__. Per Annum but this may be helped by the Annexing to such parishes as are adjacent." They added that "for want of opportunity" many un-baptized infants had perished in the "Indian war . . . but that [the]Warr [was] now Terminated and [the] Country very likely to Flourish again in all other respects except that of religion" (Cain 240).

During the sixteen years between the 1717 appeal and John Garzia's appearance in 1733, the settlers in St. Thomas Parish remained without a permanent dedicated minister. (The brief appearances of the Reverends Mr. Baylye and Mr. Taylor had obviously failed to satisfy the religious needs of St. Thomas Parish.)

The Garzia family's move to Bath was, clearly, a significant event in the progress of the little community.

Finally an experienced priest had arrived whose reputation in the colonies was apparently without blemish, and John Garzia subsequently proved to be steadfast in his efforts to bring the gospel to St. Thomas Parish. Garzia undertook and persevered in what has to be one of the most arduous and frustrating positions imaginable for a priest.

John Garzia first arrived alone in Bath in January 1733, and then four months later he "Cast Away, going to Virginia for My Family from Aprill the 27 to May the 5" (Cain 353, 379). From Farnham in the Northern Neck of Virginia, the Garzias traveled to Bath by boat, the only practical method for family travel in that period. During the four months in Bath prior to returning to Farnham for Mary and their three children, John Garzia was, without doubt, making arrangements for his family's new life. (Where the Garzia family first lived when they came to Bath is not known.) At that time daughters Katherine and Jane were thirteen and twelve years old, and son John was two years old.

Garzia plunged himself into his ministry in Bath: in just a year following the new parson's move to Bath, he was involved in the construction of St. Thomas Church. The vestry members and their rector intended that their church building should be built sound enough to remain intact for future generations, as indeed it has to this day. The walls of the nearly rectangular structure are two feet thick brick set in Flemish bond, and they have withstood devastating storms, periods of neglect, and the considerable ravages of time. The tiles of the floor were set in sand, as was the custom, to allow the burial of parishioners within the sanctity of the church, and a balcony was included to accommodate the slaves belonging to some of the worshipers below.[2] At the time of its completion, St. Thomas Church was the only church in the province where Anglican services were being held, and Garzia was one of just three Anglican clergymen in the entire colony (Angley 53).

Saint Thomas Church

Bath, North Carolina, 2003. Photograph Courtesy of Michael Mansfield.

In 1735, two and a half years after the Garzias' move to Bath, John Garzia bought three lots and erected a dwelling on them. The Garzia home was on the north-east edge of town, near the town limits of present day Bath (Beaufort Co. Deeds. Bk. 2 72-73).[3] In the same year the Crown granted Garzia a large tract of land across the Pamlico River from Bath Town (Hoffman 4).[4] Regrettably Garzia was never able to cultivate his land. (At that time it is unlikely that he had either the financial or human capital required for such an undertaking. At the time of his death he still owned his home and land, though they were encumbered by debt.)

The Provincial legislature regulated the established church by a series of "Vestry Acts." These statutes created Anglican parishes and determined the makeup of a vestry with regard to qualifications, tenure, and range of duties. The statutes also outlined the expected services of parish priests and established minimum compensation by their vestries. To defray the costs of erecting and maintaining church buildings, purchasing of glebe lands, and paying clerical salaries, taxes were established. In addition, various fines for wrongdoing were, in part, designated for the use of the parish.[5] Furthermore vestries themselves were empowered to levy a yearly tax of up to five shillings on all "tithables" in the parish. According to the provisions of these Vestry Acts, John Garzia was required to officiate at a church or chapel in the parish at least ten Sundays per year, and he was to be paid at least £50 annually for his services (Cain xxv-xx).[6] Gifts of commodities from parishioners constituted another potential source of parochial upkeep.

The St. Thomas Parish vestry members were evidently pleased to have Mr. Garzia in their midst and were eager for him to remain. But whether due to the general scarcity of money in the province or to a parsimonious disposition, Garzia's vestry did not meet the Vestry Act's minimum salary requirements for the support of its rector. In fact, although he probably received gifts of commodities such as foods and household necessities, it is clear in Garzia's letters that there were years on end when he received no salary whatsoever. To make ends meet, Garzia was forced to depend on the savings he had brought with him from Virginia.[7] This state of financial affairs prompted letters to the Bishop of London The Right Rev. Mr. Gibson, from both the St. Thomas Vestry and from Garzia in 1735.

The vestry's letter[8] (See Appendix E) requested that the Bishop forward and promote the enclosed petition (addressed to Bishop Gibson) from Garzia. In their letter the members of the vestry also requested the bishop's intercession with the SPG on the behalf of St. Thomas Parish. It stated that the vestry was "destitute of means . . . to allow a decent maintenance for a protestant Minister by reason of our poverty" to which the "late Massacre, and severe persecution of the Savage Indian Nations bordering upon us have not a little contributed." The vestry declared that "we are encourag'd to retain the said Reverend Minister (Garzia); but to our extreme grief, the maintenance that we by reason of our poverty can afford him, is far short of our inclinations in Supporting decently a man of his worth and merit." The vestry added that "we are now building at our own proper Costs a Small Church (being the only one in the whole province)" (Cain 353-54).

Garzia's letter (See Appendix F) to his patron, Bishop Gibson, requested that the bishop intercede with the SPG with a request for books, furnishings, and "Other conveniencies as your Lordship shall think proper (all being wanting)" for his church. Though construction was not complete, there is ample evidence in Garzia's letter that as soon as the walls and roof were installed, St. Thomas Church was put to use for worship. In a more distinctly clerical aside in the letter, Garzia added that, though he was pleased with the efforts of his parishioners, he believed some of their profane behavior needed correction (Cain 357-58).

Garzia's communications included another, more personal letter to the Bishop requesting Bishop Gibson's intercession with the SPG (See Appendix G). In this second letter Garzia reiterated his appeal for financial support. He observed that his vestry had not been able to meet even the minimum salary designated by the vestry laws and his own meager savings were shrinking. In this petition Garzia presented his resumé with a request that the Society would help support him with a "remission to be made to the Governor as well for my past services, as for my future maintenance." (Garzia's request for financial assistance also clearly implied that he desired to be appointed a missionary of the SPG.) In this letter Garzia also urged that more clergy be sent to the region. Obviously there was a need for assistance in ministering to the scattered inhabitants of the province and this isolated priest must have longed for the fellowship of a brother clergyman (Cain 358-59).

On May 8, 1735, the same date as his letters to the Bishop of London, Garzia also wrote directly to the SPG (See Appendix H). [9] He requested that the Society honor its financial commitment concerning the baptism of slaves in the colonies. Garzia informed the Society that it he had complied with instructions and, while in Virginia, did "Baptize and instruct severall Negroes as [it] appears by the List hereto annext." He had previously reported this activity to the Society and he was now requesting that the Society "be pleased to transmitt for the said service such an allowance As to you shall seem meet" (Cain 357).

At about the same time that Garzia was purchasing his three lots and erecting his family's dwelling (1735), a particularly significant event occurred in the eventful life of John Garzia. He was chosen to officiate for Governor Gabriel Johnston and the Assembly at Edenton. No doubt John Garzia's satisfaction with his participation in the event was enhanced when, later, he was paid a very handsome honorarium A legislative dispatch gives the details:

>TO THE HONOURABLE THE UPPER HOUSE,
>
>In the Lower House Tuesday February the 11th 1734. [1735]
>
>Resolved that the sum of Twenty pounds be paid out of the Publick Treasury unto the Reverend Mr John Garsia, for performing divine Service and preaching a Sermon before his Excellency ye Governour Council and Assembly Sunday last; and that His Excellency be desired to issue his Warrant for payment thereof.
>
>Sent to the Upper House for Concurrance by Mr Turner
>
>Mr Roberts.
>
>Which was concurred with.
>
>By Order   JOS. ANDERSON, C^{lk} Gen Ass (Saunders 92).

There was also another occasional source of income for Garzia. As was previously mentioned, various fines in the provisions of the Vestry Acts were designated for distribution to the clergy and parishes. For instance, the Act of 1715 provided that "no lay person in any parish where a minister or priest is resident shall join any person in marriage under the penalty of five pounds. One half to the parish for the Use of the poor and the other to the Minister resident or incumbent." In March 1735 Parson Garzia, enforced this law to his benefit in court. He informed on and testified against a Justice of the Peace, Henry Crofton, who had joined Andrew Lathinghouse and Patience Smith in marriage, and the court found for plaintiff, Garzia (Cain 364).

These additional sources of income were, without doubt, welcome but hardly met the Garzia family's needs, and the family remained destitute. Almost a year after the foregoing appeals, Garzia had still not heard from the SPG. Accordingly, in a letter dated March 1736, he again asked Bishop Gibson to deliver to the SPG the enclosed request that Garzia be appointed a missionary of the Society in order to help his poor parish support him:

> May it please yr. Lordship
> In the month of May 1735 I made bold to send to your Lordship two Petitions at the request of my vestry, one to your Lordship and the other to the society for propagating the Gospell in foreign pts. Humbly begging your Lordships intercession with the society to enter me into the list of Missionaries in order to help this poor parish to support me their minister, their poverty being so great that of themselve's, they are

not able. I have for the use of our new church being the only one in this Government; and have also sent the attestation of Mr. Comissary Blair and the Governor of Virga. As touching my life and conversation during my abode there for about nine years, together with an account of my proceedings pursuant to the instructions of the society by doctor thos. Bray in relation to the instructing and baptizing the negros in Virga. their Number being upwards of three hundred as by the said account appears; I hope, that the said Petitions and letters are come to your Lordship's hands, but not having heard any thing about them, Embolden's me thus to reiterate my indigence and necessity, as having but £200 of this currency[10] which answers about £20 sterling, which is far short to support me and my family, (cloathing being very scarce and dear) and my self at present very much in want; Our present Governor Mr. Johnston has ever since his first coming (pursuant to your Lordships letter to him) used his best endeavours to have a Competent maintenance settled on the clergy, but the majority of the assembly being so ill dispos'd that he cant but lament his incapacity, as yet to compleat so good a work. I humbly beg your Lordship answer directed to his Excellency the Governor and craving your Lordship blessing, and praying for your Lordships prosperity as

well spirituall as temporall, (well remembering the past Kindness and benefits I recd. at your Lordships hands) I remain your Lordship's Most dutifull son, and Most obedient humble Servant.
John Garzia
No. Carolina, Bath town
St. thos. Parish March 19 th, 1735 [36]
[Endorsed]
Received June 1736
Read at the Society 17 Septr. 1736
Ordered a Church Bible and Common Prayer book be sent him, and that he be acquainted the Society are not in a condition to establish new missions (Cain 364-65).

Garzia's letter to the SPG which was enclosed in the one to Bishop Gibson stated that Garzia had sent two previous requests[11] that he be entered into the list of SPG missionaries "that by that means I might be supported." He further stated that, as he had not "as yet heard any thing in answer thereto I humbly beg the favour of you to Signifie to me the resolution of the Society in relation to that affair" (Cain 366).

All that John Garzia accomplished, as a result of these appeals, was that he was sent a Bible and a Book of Common Prayer and the news that "the Society are not in a condition to establish New Missions" (Cain 366). What a blow this must have been to Garzia and his vestry. The congregation would have to sustain itself with the meager resources which could be garnered locally. So they struggled on as best they could, and nothing was heard from St. Thomas Parish for the next few years.

The next recorded event in the life of the parson was a letter with news of a box of books that had been sent to Garzia by way of the Bishop of London's Commissary, the Reverend Mr. Alexander Garden in Charleston [12] In response to Mr. Garzia's inquiries concerning the books, he received the following terse note from Mr. Garden:

> Your 2d Letter, concerning a Box of Books for you from the Society, is come to hand, in which you mention 3 former ones you had wrote me, one of which only I have recd., desiring me to find an Opportunity of sending the said Box to Edenton consigned to Governor Johnson.
>
> The said Box has been in my Custody nigh a 12 month and you may wait 7 years before any such opportunity offers as from hence to Edenton. And I must acquaint you, that it must be your Business to look after for such Opportunity from that Place Hither, and by such to send me your Order for the Delivery to some particular Person.
>
> I am your very humble Servant.
>
> A. Garden
>
> [Addressed]
> To The Reverend Mr. Garzia Minister
> at Bath town
> North Carolina (Cain 378).

Though one of the duties of Garden's position was to see to the well-being of clergymen in the Carolinas, his tone, as suggested by this letter, would indicate that he was neither humble nor interested in the condition of clergymen in his charge.

In May 1738, probably as a result of his previously mentioned alcoholic excess, the newly appointed SPG missionary in North Carolina, the Rev. Mr. John Boyd (the former Virginia doctor) died. Governor Johnston who had recognized the worthiness of John Garzia and was aware of his destitute state recommended Garzia for the vacant SPG missionary post. In June 1738 the governor sent the following letter, along with Garzia's own account of his clerical efforts in the province, to the SPG

> To the Honorable the Lords and Gentlemen of the Society for propagating the Christian Religion in forreing parts

> The Reverend Mr. John Boyd the Missionary for this Province having dyed the 19 or 20th Day of May and having in this Province a worthy and Religious poor Minister the reverend John Garzia of St. Thomas's Parish Pamptico Incumbent who before my coming to this Province the People of that Parish induced by fair Promises to come from Virginia and live among them and at present they are willing to Starve with his Wife and three Children by not paying him his little Sallery for Two Years and a half past which knowing and likewise his indefatiguable care in going often from Parish to Parish preaching the Word of God and Baptizing as will appear by his Report In Consideration of which I do recommend him to yr. Honorable Society to Be ap-

pointed a Missionary for this Province being not only a fit person but the Same will be an Act of Charity to the relief of him from the Oppression he labours under and if So I desire an Answer to inform him of his Duty therein.
Yr. Honors Most Obedient Servant.
Gab. Johnston (Cain 384).

As an accompaniment to Governor Johnston's letter, Garzia sent the Society "A True Account of the number of People Baptized by me [Reverend John Garzia] In this Province from the Year of Our Lord 1733 to this Present 1738 with the Names of the Parishes and Precincts." This impressive account listed John Garzia's efforts, not just in his home parish, but in visits throughout the province of North Carolina. He traveled to preach and baptize repeatedly in the distant settlements of "Society Parish Bartie Precinct", "Hide Precinct", "Edenton Parish Chowan Precinct", "Cuscopnung River Saint Andrews Parish Tarrel Precinct", "Newbern Town Craven Precinct", "Old and new Mattummuskete", "Aligator Creek Saint Andrews Parish","Carteret Precinct", "Onslo Precinct", and "Newhannover Precinct." On his own initiative, and without supervision or sponsorship, this extraordinarily dedicated man repeatedly undertook difficult visits by boat or horseback to the colony's widely scattered settlements. He visited some of them more than once annually. In the document he sent to the Society, he listed those persons baptized by year and by location, and he separated his counts of males and females. In those 5 1/2 years he had baptized 918 men and 839 women for a total of 1,757 souls — all in locations *outside* of St. Thomas

Parish. In his home parish, St. Thomas, he had baptized 279 men and 242 women (Cain 378-80).

Garzia's letters of recommendation from Governor Johnston and from the Bishop of London, as well as Garzia's own account of his visitations for preaching and baptism, were read at meetings of the SPG, and in May and June 1738, it was agreed "that Mr. Garzia be appointed Missionary to North Carolina in the Room of Mr. Boyd deceased with a Salary of £50 per Annum, to Commence from Michaelmas last" (Cain 397).

The secretary to the SPG, the Reverend Philip Bearcroft, in compliance with the Society's foregoing decision, wrote Mr. Garzia and Governor Johnston:

> To the Reverend Mr. Garzia of North Carolina.
>
> Reverend Sir
>
> The Society for the Propagation of the Gospel in Foreign Parts hath rec'd. your Petition to succeed Mr. Boyd in his Mission together with the Acct. of yr. Religious Services in North Carolina and out of regard to them and the recommendation of Governor Johnson hath appointed you to succeed Mr. Boyd in his Mission with a Salary of £50 per Annum to commence so far Back as Michaelmas last, so that you may draw as soon as you please for what Salary is due to you on Messrs. Wm. And Thos. Tryon Merchants in Crutched Fryers Treasurers, to the Society, the Society some time since appointed Mr. Moir their Missionary, when he shall arrive in the Province you will shew all Brotherly Love

and Kindness to him, and jointly as well as separately endeavour to the very best of your Power to propagate and promote the most Holy Religion of our great Lord and Saviour Jesus Christ. I have inclosed a Notitia Parochialis to which you are to conform, as far as the Circumstances of yr. Mission will permit and transmit every half Year an Account of yr. Labours to Sir
P.B.
Aug. 28th 1739 (Cain 397).

The foregoing letter to Garzia was enclosed in Secretary Bearcroft's letter to Governor Johnston. The governor was informed that Mr. Garzia had been appointed a missionary of the SPG. The communication further stated that the province had been divided into two missionary districts. Mr. Garzia was assigned the district north and east of the Neuse and that the Rev. Mr. James Moir would assume the duties of missionary in the division south and west of the Neuse. It was explained that Mr. Moir was replacing Mr. Marsden, who had been appointed missionary to that division, but "upon his misbehavior and a further Inquiry into his Character the Society have dismissed him their Service" (Cain 397). [13]

Soon after the SPG appointed Garzia a missionary, Secretary Bearcroft wrote "St. Pauls Parish, Chowan and Elsewhere"[14] to inform the inhabitants of Mr. Garzia's appointment and to recommend that toll-free ferry passage be procured for him.

London, Warwick Court
Warwick Lane, Nov. 19 1739
Gentlemen,

I am directed by the incorporated Society for the Propagation of the Gospel in Foreign Parts to acquaint you, that they have appointed the Reverend Mr. John Garzia to be one of their Missionaries in North Carolina, and that he Officiates in Chowan Precinct, and in all other places as Occasion require to the North East side of the River Neuse. The Society do hereby Recommend him to yr. Favour, and as he is very sufficently Recommended to them, more Especially by his Excellency Gabriel Johnston Esqr., they conceive good hopes he will answer the End of his Mission; and they do Expect you will Contribute, according to the best of yr. Ability, towards his better Support, and Recommend it to you to procure him a Passage Toll-Free, in the Several Ferries over the Rivers within his Mission. Praying, that you may make a right Use, of having the great blessing of Gods word administred to you, and that it may Shine forth in yr. Lives and Conversations. I am, Gentlemen, Yr. Humble Servant.

Philip Bearcroft
[Plea]se to Direct thus,
The Inhabitants of St. Paul's Parish, Chowan, and of all other Places where I [sic] shall officiate (Saunders 560)

This letter was delivered to the lower house (the popular or elective branch) of the Assembly in August 1740, and that legislative body taking into Consideration the Letter from the society for propogating the Gospel in foreign Parts, recommending Mr Garzia to have free Passage over the Rivers within his Mission, have Resolved, that all Missionaries within this Province, pass free from paying any Money, for their Ferrage over the Rivers within their respective Missions, And that the several Persons who keep such Ferrys, shall have a claim on and be paid by the Publick for such service. To which Wee desier your Hon^{rs} Concurrence.

The upper house (the governor and his appointed council) concurred with the resolution on August 21, 1740 (Saunders 571).

The next recorded reference to Garzia was by George Whitefield in July 1741. Whitefield, an Anglican minister, was one of the first circuit-riding missionary preachers, and he was the personification of the "Great Awakening" in colonial America. This remarkable man was one of the principal founders of Methodism, though he later broke with John Wesley and became a rigid Calvinist. In a long and learned letter to the Bishop of Oxford, Whitefield (who held most of the Anglican clergymen of colonial America in contempt) reported that on

> looking over the list of the Missionaries, that there are no less than twenty employed in preaching and teaching school in [the province] of New England (where certainly the Gospel is preached to greater purity than at home) and but two settled Missionaries in all North-Carolina and one of

those viz. Mr. Garzia, can scarce speak English. Does not this look too much like making a Party of Religion? (Cain 423).

In his reply to Whitefield, the Bishop of Oxford pointed out that Whtefield had exhibited a tendency to be severely uncharitable in assessments of his fellow clergy in England and abroad. The Bishop added that it was very difficult to induce missionaries to go to North Carolina in particular, because of "the bad Reception of those who were sent" (Cain 426).

Legend has it that Whitefield was so contemptuous of his reception during one of his visits to Bath Town that on leaving, he shook the dust from his feet and issued the curse that the village would never grow.[15]

In April 1741 John Garzia sent a narrative report (See Appendix I) and his mandated periodic *notitia parochialis*[16] to the Secretary of the SPG. Garzia opened his report with his "humble Thanks to the Honorable Society for propagating the Christian Knowledge in Forreign parts, having appointed me one of their Missionarys" and for their "great Charity in appointing me Sallery for the Preceding Years." He wrote that he had mailed his report in the preceding year, but that he had recently learned that the ship carrying his mail had been captured by the Spanish, and consequently the report was never delivered. He wrote that he had "demanded of Mrs. Boyd Relict of my Predecessor [the widow of the deceased missionary whom Garzia replaced] the books belonging to the mission, according to order; but received only a bible in Folio, a Common Prayer Book, the Book of Homelies and Doctor Tillotsons Sermons Three Volumes; for which I gave a receipt, as for the rest She can only say, that her Husband frequently lent them out and all her Endeavours to find them Seem ineffectual." Garzia also wrote that the "House orderd me to have passage Ferry free, over the Severall Rivers and Creeks within my mission at the Expense of the Publick." He continued that he had read the Society's letter directing congregations that Garzia visited to help defray his travel expenses, but that "So far (I am sorry to say it) are the People here from contributing to the Advancement of the Glory of God" and that "my traveling expenses will not be less than five pound Sterling per Annum." Garzia continued "I pray you Sir to recommend to their Lordships and honors to Send me Some Monitors against Swearing, Drunkeness, and breach of the Sabbath also preparatorys for worthyly approching the Lords Table; and if possible a few Spelling Books for the Erudition of poor Children within my Mission; and farther pray, that a Silver Cup with the Hutch and Plate of any other Proper Metal, for the decent Administring the Lords Supper, may be added, at my own Expence payable out of my Sallery, with the Name of the Donor" (Cain 420-21).

The *notitia parochialis* (See Appendix J) which accompanied Garzia's narrative report estimated the population in Garzia's mission to be 9000 souls. He recorded that he had baptized 519 in the parish since he was appointed a missionary but that the number of actual communicants in St. Thomas Parish was twenty-seven, and within the mission — exclusive of the parish — seventy-two.

Garzia's foregoing reports were read at a meeting of the SPG five months later, at which time it was agreed that Garzia be sent 40 shillings worth of the tracts he had requested. It was also agreed "that the said Letter be referred back to the Committee for their further Consideration, and that it be referred to the said Committee to consider of a more Effectual Method for the better preservation of the Libraries of the Missionaries" (Cain 421). The Society sent the chalice as John Garzia had requested, and the cost was deducted from his pay. However Garzia never saw his chalice. To the Society's credit, it had been sent, in due time, to Commissary Garden at Charles Town in South Carolina to be transmitted to Garzia. However, the chalice did not reach Bath until 1747, three years after Garzia's death. At that time it was placed in the hands of Mary Garzia by none other than the Rev. George Whitefield (Angley 52). Parson Garzia would undoubtedly have been thrilled with his silver chalice which bears the inscription *D D Johannes Garzia Ecclesia Anglicana.*[17]

The Garzia Chalice

John Garzia's Chalice was delivered to Mary Garzia by the Reverend George Whitestone three years after John Garzia's death. The chalice is still in use at St. Thomas Church today. It bears the inscription *D D Johannes Garzia Ecclesia Anglicana.* Photograph courtesy of Michael Mansfield.

Various reports to the SPG and the Bishop of London give a glimpse of the activities and character of John Garzia. Though he had to endure deprivation, disappointments and physical hardships, he remained a steadfast and dutiful pastor to the 9000 settlers that he estimated were living in his jurisdiction. He not only promoted the building of St. Thomas Church by his presence, but he probably labored in its physical construction. Not only did he preach and baptize in his church, but he traveled extensively to deliver these services to the settlers of northeastern North Carolina. He persevered in these travels despite the realization that, contrary to the directions of his ecclesiastic superiors, the settlers he visited would not help defray his expenses. He was genuinely troubled by the profanity, drunkenness, and irreverence that prevailed in his flock, and he sought means to improve these general behaviors. The lack of educational opportunities for children also concerned him, and he attempted to acquire educational materials through the SPG.[18]

The corpus of John Garzia's correspondence from colonial America is illuminating and of great interest. Like his communications from Dublin, the hand writing, spelling, and idiomatic style of composition of the letters actually suggest another scribal hand. It is highly unlikely that John, who, even then was not very proficient with the English language, wrote them. Though the information in these documents obviously originated with John, the actual writer and composer must have been his wife Mary.

The final existing document attributed to John Garzia is his report to the SPG dated April 16, 1742. From it the reader learns that when Garzia as the SPG-appointed missionary began receiving a regular salary from the Society in London, his vestry saw an opportunity to stop contributing to his support. Consequently, when this last report was written, Garzia had received no salary from his parish for about four years, and he had resorted to legal action against his vestry. The Garzia family remained poor, and the meager family savings were being consumed by living expenses and by legal fees. Garzia's frustration and discouragement are evident in this last known communication to the Secretary of the SPG:

>NO CAROLINA
>BATH TOWN
>April 16: 1742.

REVEREND SIR

In obedience to the order of the honorable Society to me I send by this a true and faithful account of my services for this year from this time twelve months Viz^t

The number baptized by me in my Resident Parish and all other within my Mission, which are Six hundred and twenty three, beside nine adults and three negroes.

The number of the communicants in all, as above are one hundred and three.

As to the number of those who profess themselves of the Church of England Dissenters & Papists I cannot as yet send you an account thereof.

The number of Heathen & Infidels I am informed amount to two thousand or thereabouts.

I do beg the favour of you to inform their Honours with my endeavours, to promote goodness, christianity and the true Religion among the Inhabitants within my mission, but immorality is arrived to that head among so many, that it requires not only some time but great patience to conquer it; because upon my preaching upon any prevalent & predominant Sin, I must be prepared to stand the persecution of those who are guilty of it, especially in my resident Parish, in which adultery, Incest, Blasphemy, and all kinds of profaneness has got such deep root.

I shall be more large in my next, In the mean time I stand the oppression of an inveterate and obstinate Parish, govern'd by twelve Vestry men, whose only endeavour is to hinder & obstruct the service of God, being performed, they themselves never coming to hear the word of God, and dissuading as much as possible others from it and who in a particular manner exercise their malice daily against me, by depriving me of per ann[m] allow'd by law, & which I am obliged to have recourse to recover, having had nothing these 4 years for the support of my Family, but what is allow'd to me by the Hon[ble] Society, for whom my humble Prayers to God, & my humble respect to your Reverence & begging the continuance of your favour, am

Rev[d] Sir, your most, &c.,
JOHN GARZIA (Saunders 604-05)

John Garzia's frustration is understandable, but, in all fairness, there were obviously a number of good, well-meaning parishioners in St. Thomas Parish during his ministry there. After all, they had dedicated themselves to the formidable task of building St. Thomas Church, which at the time, was the finest public structure in the province of North Carolina. And, at least some of them attended services, as Garzia's reports to his superiors indicate. It is likely that these people also contributed to the material welfare of the Garzia family. It is reasonable to assume that Garzia had help with the construction of his home and that the Garzias were supported with gifts of food and other necessities. Otherwise the Garzia family would have been in danger of starvation, at times, considering the expenses of the minister's missionary travel and the persistant lack of vestry support.

John Garzia's eventful life ended abruptly two years later in 1744 while on his way to visit the sick, when he was killed by a fall from a horse. It is believed that he is buried under the tiles of the floor of the church he had helped build and where he had presided for eleven years.

Like many noteworthy men of the church, John Garzia had checkered beginnings, but in one of the most challenging assignments imaginable, he redeemed himself admirably. His life was truly a journey from sinner to saint.

These are they who have come out of the great ordeal;
They have washed their robes and made them white in the blood of the Lamb.
For this reason they are before
The throne of God,
And worship him day and night

within his temple,
and the one who is seated on the throne will shelter them.
They will hunger no more, and
thirst no more;
the sun will not strike them,
nor any scorching heat;
for the Lamb at the center of the
throne will be their
shepherd,
and he will guide them to
springs of the water of life,
and God will wipe away every
 tear from their eyes.

    Revelation 7. 14-17 (NRSV Bible).

Epilogue

John Garzia's death left his widow, Mary, and their three children in dire circumstances. They were without benefit of further SPG salary, and John's efforts to obtain — through legal channels — his much overdue parish salary had exhausted the family's savings. By then daughters Katherine and Jane were 26 and 25 years old; son John was 13 years old.

John Garzia's death was reported to the Society by Mary in the first of several letters pleading for assistance. She wrote this first letter on Christmas Eve 1744:

> Rev. Sir
> My husband the reverend John Garzia is dead and I am left a poor widow in a strange land with not anything to live upon my condition is veri deplorable. Foreign goods and provisions are veri dear in this place since the war[1] the salary this contri allows the clergy is a triffle and that veri ill paid Mr. Garzia was forced to go to law for it and recovered it but is not yet paid he died of a fall of his horse as he was comin at some distance from home . . . Pray good Sr be so good as to lay these few lines before the honorable Society and i humbly beg their lordships will please to answer a poor minister's widow so as to help me to

get over my troubles which are very great at this time (Angley 57).

There is a hint in the following letter to the Society from their new missionary, the Rev. Clement Hall, that Mary and the children had developed some occupation that might sustain them if they had financial help with reclaiming their property. On July 9, 1748, Hall wrote the Society:

> I learn that the widow Garzia is but in low circumstances, chiefly by reason of her deceased's Husband's Expenses & trouble in sueing for his Dues which occasioned him to be very much behind hand in the world & ye creditors of late have sold all both Lands & Houses. She returns hearty thanks to ye Honble Society for their former bounty to her and desires to know whether there is anything allow'd yearly for the Missionaries Widows — Since the war commenced Goods are excessively dear & besides ye Industry of herself & children she hath but little to support herself withal. She humbly prays ye Worthy Society to consider her helpless condition & allow her some further supply as they shall think proper, whereby she may be enabled to redeem her Lotts and Houses and to maintain herself and three children (with their own care and Industry) from Penury & contempt (Saunders 872).

In May of 1749, Mary Garzia again wrote the SPG. Evidently she had received some assistance from the Society, for which she expressed gratitude. But she asked that additional assistance be given so that she and her children might "not perish in a strange land." By this time Mary had lost the house that her husband had built, and she was renting from the same creditors who had seized it (Angley 58). The minutes of its meeting of April 17, 1751, reveal that the Society considered another of Mary Garzia's appeals:

> A letter from Mrs. Garzia, Widow of Mr. Garzia, late one of the missionaries in North Carolina, Dated Bath Town in North Carolina, Jan. 8 1750/51, setting forth that her condition was so very deplorable, that she had not at that time a Farthing to relieve her wants, and that she had already sold almost all her goods out of mere necessity for subsistence, having lost her health for 12 months past, and was in danger of having her Bed taken from under her, that she must utterly perish, if not relieved by the Society, which she hopes out of their great goodness will grant some present relief to help her pay her small debts and keep her from starving.

The Society agreed that the Reverend Clement Hall should "make a particular Enquiry into the Circumstances of Mrs. Garzia, and if he finds her in the condition represented in her Letter, he be Impowered, to relieve her as far as five pounds" (Angley 58).

The last known record of Mary Garzia was a letter from the new rector of St. Thomas Church, the Rev. Alexander Stewart who arrived in Bath in the fall of 1753 — nine years after John Garzia's death.[2] Stewart saw fit to inform the Society that Mary Garzia was "really an Object of Charity." According to Mary's own letter, which accompanied Stewart's, the creeping infirmities of age and approaching blindness were adding to her misery. Again, perhaps for the last time, the Society "Resolved to give Mrs. Garzia the Sum of Five Pounds" (Angley 59).

Notwithstanding their impoverished state, either Mary or her children were able by means which have not been recorded to regain possession of their Bath property.

No additional record of the oldest Garzia child, Katherine has been discovered.

Jane Garzia remained in North Carolina. In June 1757, Mr. Charles Forbes applied to the Beaufort County Court "to have a bastard child sworn to him by Jane Garzia now under her care removed, whereupon it ordered that a Summons issue for the said Jane to appear next Court and answer thereto." In December of 1757, Jane who was then 39 years old appeared in court as summoned and she "exhibited her acdt. Of her lying in and maintenance of a bastard child agst. Charles Forbes father thereof . . . ordered by the Court that the said Charles Forbes pay the same" (Angley endnote 191). Nothing further is known concerning Jane or her child.

The youngest Garzia child, son John who listed his occupation as "mariner" moved to Rhode Island. He distinguished himself by serving as a Captain and Paymaster in Colonel Robert Elliot's Rhode Island Regiment during the Revolutionary War. Garzia married Esther Thomas and they had at least one daughter named Anna. The 1790 census listed John Garzia in East Greenwich Town, Rhode Island, and living with six females. In the year 1795, when he was 65 years old, John returned to Beaufort County and sold the Garzia home site as well as the property on South Creek (Beaufort Co. Deeds. Bk 7 84).

Anna Garzia married Edward Weeden in 1815 and they had sixteen children. At least eight of the Weeden children lived to become adults, and the Weeden descendents of John Garzia number in the hundreds.

Appendices

Appendix A
Trial of the Nuns February 6, 1719
The Whole Tryal and Examination of Anne Crofford, Mary Smith, Jane Sexton, and Mary Chivers, four Nunns, who were Try'd at the King's Bench this 6th Day of February, 1718,[1] for Remaining in this Kingdom, contrary to the Statutes; also the Second Taryal and Examination of Richard Wilson

The first Evidence for the King against the said Nuns was John Garzee, who being sworn said, that in the Month of October, 1718, the said Garsee was several Times at Mass in Channel-Row, at the Dutchess of Tyrconnels, that Mass was Celebrated in a House or Chappel of Ease commonly call'd the Nunnery, that he took particular Notice of the Traversers, and several other Young Women, who are reputed Nunns, in a part of the said Nunnery, by themselves at Mass; and that he very well knew them to be Nunns for several Reasons: The Court ask'd him what reasonable Circumstances he could show, to prove that they were Nunns; who made Answer, That he was sensible that every young Woman who took the Vow of Chastity, and became a Nunn, had in a Year's time a Ring bestowed upon her, and a knotted Cord, called a St. Francis's Girdle, and that he knew every one of the Traversers to have the like; and he likewise knew them severally to have used a prayer that is not used by any others, but such as are Nuns; the court ask'd him if other persons were not allow'd to say that Prayer as well as Nunns, and what sort of a Prayer it was, who answer'd that there was three Psalms and three Prayers which they Daily used, and were oblig'd punctually to observe.

The court ask'd him what sort of Cloaths or Habit they wore and whether they were the usal Habit of Nunns, who said that they were Black and White that when they came abroad, they left that Black and White at Hom, and went like any other Gentlewomen for fear of being Discover'd and that they severally told him that they could weare the usual Habits of Nunns as in other Countries, if it were not for the Prosecution that is over them: The Court ask'd him if they severally behave themselves and perform'd their Devotion as Nunns do in other Countries, who Answered that they did the very same way, and he further said, that the said Crofford was an Abbiss and so Reputed and Respected by all the rest, and that all the rest of the Gentlewomen call'd her Mother. The Court ask'd him if he thought that they call'd her Mother after a Religious manner or after what other manner, who Answer'd that he was sure it was after a Religious manner, and as being an Abbess, and no other.

Sir Theobald Butler, and Councellor Darcy being Councils for the Traversers they desired the Court to ask'd Garsee if any Novice or any other Person, might not say and use the Prayer as the Traversers did, and were a Ring and Girdle as they did, who Answer, that they must first obtaine a Dispensation for so doing. Sir Theobald said that the said Crawford was a Married Wife and desired that Garsee may be Examined if ever he knew or heard so, which Garsee being ask'd, he declr'd he was told she was a Widdow the Court ask'd him, if it was Lawful for a Widdow after the Death of her Husband to become Nunn or Abbess, who said that it may be very Lawful as well as for a Man to become a Priest after the Death of his Wife.

The said Garsee being a Spaniard and could speak no English, he was examined by and interpreter, one Mr. Ducas a Minister.

The second Evidence for the King was one Mrs. Sergeant, wife to Mr. George Sergeant, High Constable of this City, who being Sworn, said, that when the Traversers were apprehended, she was employ'd to Search and Examine them, and said that she found a pair of Beads and a Ring in Mrs. Smith's Pocket, and that she likewise found a knotted Cord about her Body on the outside of her Shift; and that she found another pair of Beads, a prayer Book and a small Crucifix in the said Mrs. Sexton's Pocket, and another Cord about her Body on the outside of her Shift; but that she found nothing with the other two, neither did she remember that she saw them; Mrs. Sergeant produc'd the aforesaid things in Court, which were view'd by the judges and several others in Court.

The third Evidence was Mr. George Sergeant, who being sworn, said that about 2 a-Clock in the Morning he was rais'd out of Bed by the late Sheriffs, with whom he went to the Dutchess of Tyrconnel's, where he saw two of the Traversers, who he knew, because they came along with him in a Coach to Judge Caulfields House; but the other two he could not Swear to, because they were along with the Sheriffs in another Coach.

The fourth Evidence for the King was the late Sheriff Reazon who being Sworn, said that by Order of the Government he went to the Nunnery in Channel Row, where he saw a great many Women, whereof he brought four to Judge Caulfields, which he believed to be the Traversers.

One Mr. Garvey was examin'd in behalf of Mrs. Crafford about her being Married, who upon his Oath, said, that he had known the said Crafford for about 20 years past, and that about twelve Years ago he was inform'd that she was Married to one Mr. Crafford; but that he never knew nor saw her Husband, that he at several time went to visit the Traverser at the Dutchess of Tyrconnel's but did never hear any Body say that she was a Nun or an Abbess; the Court ask'd the Transvsers what they had to say for themselves, or if they had any Witnesses to produce, the said Crafford said that Garsee Swore against her, but was false as God is true; but that they had no Witnesses but God Almighty; after the Tryal was over, the said Garsee went off well guarded by one of the Messengers, a Sergeant and 10 soldiers, who waited in court during the time of the tryal; they Jury having receiv'd the charge, brought in their Verdict, that the said Mrs. Smith and Sexton were Guilty, and the other two not Guilty.

The said Smith and Sexton are to be transported. Wilson was tried for Stealing a Case of Pistols from Councellor Doyne, but after a short tryal was brought in not Guilty.

Dublin, Printed by R.D (Wake Letters 13: 44 (2)).

Appendix B
Garzia's letter to the Lords Justices March 1719

To their Excellencies the Lords Justices and Councill

The Humble Petition of John Garzia

Humbly Sheweth

That yo[r.] Pet[r] is a Native of Spain, and was bredd up A popish priest, and in that profession continued til he came into this Kingdom some Months agoe, When he was converted to the Protestant Religion in which he continues, and in that faith will Die

That During his continuance in the Popish Religion While in the City of Dublin, he became acquainted with Most of Popish Regular and Seculer Clergie and After his Conversion, in June last, gave Sev[ll] Exam[ons.] Before the Hon[ble] M[r] Justice Caulfield against them,. upon which Severall of them both Regulers & Seculers who Celebrated Mass tho not qualified, were taken and bound over to the last terme, but on Affid[ts.] Made by Some of them their trials were put of till

Next term and your pet^r is bound over to Prosecute them then.

That Since the said Popish Clergymen were so Apprehended great rewards have been Offer'd Yo^r Pet^r if he wou'd decline prosecuting them Which he alwais Strenuously refused to Comply with and is fully resolved to remain in this Kingdom till the said tryals are over.

That the Papists in this City, finding yor. Pet^r. determined to prosecute the popish Clergymen and that he was not to be Corupted, have frequently since last terme insulted your Pet^r. and has Contrived ways to take away his life, and perticulerly on fryday the 4th of this ins^t they in a Most barbarous Maner raised a great Mobb ag^t yor Pet^r. in James Street, Insulted, beat and much abused him, & by great Dificulty yor Pet^r. Escaped with his Life.

That your pet^r. is so threatned by them that he is afraid to walk the Streets, and is therby Deprived of All Means of Getting his bread, and the Papists give out that before next terme they will one way or Other take away your Pet^{rs} Life.

That your Pet^r would transport himself to England or some other place in his Majesties Dominions, to be safe from the fury & malice of the Papists but that he stays to prosecute the said Popish Clergymen, and in regard he canot venture himself abroad for fear of being Assassinated and that he is thereby deprived of all Means of subsisting himself, and in a deplorable Condition for want of subsistence, and that his stay here is to serve the crown and to prosecute the said Popish Clergie May it therefore please y^r Lopps (sic) to order poor Pet^r. some small Alowance to Maintain And Suport him till next terme that the said tryals are over And he will pray (MacGrath 506).

Appendix C
Governor Charles Eden's letter to SPG, October 8, 1714
North Carolina

Octor. The 8th 1715[2]

Most Honorable

The Lds. Proprietors of Carolina having thought fitt to Honour me with the Government of that part of their Lordships Province I take leave (as I think it is my Duty) to remonstrate to you the deplorable State of Religion in this poore unhappy province. It is now about four months since I enter'd upon the Goverment when I found no Clergy man upon the place except Mr. Urmstone one of your Missionarys who is realy an honest painstakeing Gentleman and worthy your Care but poore Man with utmost endeavours is not able to Serve one half of the County of Albermarle which Adjoins to Virginia, when the county of Bath of a much larger extant is wholy destitute of any Assistance I cannot find but the people are well enough inclined to embrace all oppertunitys of Attending the Service of God and to Contribute to the utmost of their Abilitys towards the support of such Missionners as you shall in Compassion to their circumstances think fit to send amongst them but our Tedious Indian Warr has reduced the Country so lowe that without your Nursing Care the very foot Steps of Religion will in a short time be worne out, and those who retains any remembrance of it will be wholy lead away by the Quakers, whereas a few of the Clergy of a Complaisant temper and Regular lives woud not only be the darlings of the people but woud be a means in time to recover those already Seduced by Quakerisme etc.

This is what I thought my Self under an Indespensible Obligationt lay before you for your Serious Consideration and at the same time I take leave t recommend to you the person from whose hands you'l receive this (Vidilicet) Mr. Thomas Gale late of Trinity Colledge in Cambridge, who I doubt not will come otherwise recommended as a very Proper person for that Service if he shall meet with your approbation.

There has been distroy'd by the Indians Since the beginning of the Warr above four Score unbaptised Infants and a great Number in the County of Bath even to Seaven years old are now under that Circumstance for noe other cause but want of Opertunity and as yet there are noe Quakers in that Country. The groth of their Sect in it I hop the Charritable care of your Most Honourable Society will effectualy prevent. I wish I cou'd be always instrumental in Serving any thing Sent by you into these parts whenever any Opertunity Offers with great readiness I shall be glad to showe how much I am Most Honourable Gentlemen your most Obedient Humble Servant.

Charles Eden (Cain 186-87).

Appendix D

Letter from the Churchwardens and Vestry of St. Thomas Parish to the SPG, March 10, 1717.

North Carolina Bath County
March the 10th 1716/17

May it Please the Honourable Society.

The great design of propogating Christian Knowledge in Forreign parts having been for these many Years past carried on with such fervency and Exemplary Success by the members of Yr. Honourable Society. It Encourages us the Subscribers members of the Vestry of St. Thomas Parish in pampicoe Humbly to recommend our present circumstances with that of the Neighbouring Parishes in Bath county to Yr.

Pious care and consideration and to Implore Yr. Further Assistance.

Wee have been told that Severall of Yr. Missionarys that have Arrived in No. Carolina were ordered by Yr. Honourable Society for this and the adjacent parishes, but as yet wee have not been so happy to have one Missionary resident in all the country and of all those that have come to No. Carolina it had been very rare that they have So much as Vizited these parts, So that many of the Children of these parts are yet unbaptized even to tenn or Twelve Years of age. Notwithstanding of which the people of this country are generally kept from dissenting from the Church of England by the care which has been taken to Appoint Readers pursuant to the Act of Assembly for Establishing the church and appointing Select Vestrys, and abstract whereof is here Inclosed, by that Act It may Easily be perceived how well inclined to the church of England the whole Government is in generall by the care taken that the Salary of the ministers shall not be less than £50.___.___ per Annum although at present there are a few of the parishes where the five Shillings per pole will not fully amount to the £50.___. Per Annum but this may be helped by the Annexing to such parishes as are adjacent till Such time as they come to be better Settled and able of themselves to make suitable provision.

Att present this is our unhappy circumstance, as well as of the other parishes in Bath county which have been Extreamly reduced by the late Indian warr In which many Scores of unbaptized Infants (who remained So for want of Oppertunity only) were barbarously Murdered but Seeing that Warr is now Terminated and our Country very likely to Flourish again in all other respects Except the only Necessary Videlicet That of religion, Wee therefore humbly beg Yr. Honourable Society will consider our present Deplorable

State and allott Some good Devine of Exemplary Life and Conversation tho of less Learning For a Missionary to these parts and wee do assure Yr. Honours Thatt wee will always make Such Further Suitable Allowance for the maintenance of Such a one as not only the laws of this Government but our own private circumstances will admitt off.

This comes by Christopher Gale Esqr. Chief Justice of No.Carolina who has been very Serviceable to these parts in promoting religious worship by whom Yr. Honourable Society may be more fully and Truly Informed of the present State and condition of these parts then it is possible for us to do in the compass of this letter.

Wee are Yr. Honours Most Obliged and Obedient, Humble Servants.
Mau. Moore Church Warden,
Thomas Worsley, Jno. Porter, John Lillington, John Adams
May it Please yr. Honours
(Endorsed:)
Church Wardens and Vestry
Of Bath County in North Carolina
March the 10th 1716/7   (Cain 240).

Appendix E

Letter from St. Thomas Parish Churchwardens and Vestry to the Bishop of London, October 10, 1734.

To the Right Reverend Father in God Edmund Lord Bishop of London.

The Humble Petition of the Church:wardens, Vestry:men and Inhabitants of St. Thomas's parish on pamlico River in the province of North Carolina.

Humbly Sheweth

That whereas Your Petitioners (notwithstanding the many sects and parties in Religion Settled amoungst us) have had the happiness of being brought up in the protestant Communion, but have been destitute of means (ever since our first Settlements) to allow a decent maintenance for a protestant Minister by reason of our poverty (to which our indigence and incapacity the late Massacre, and severe persecution of the Savage Indian Nations bordering upon us have not a little contributed).

And Whereas That ever since the first day of January 1733 (out of an ardent Zeal to encourage the protestant Religion as it is not Establish'd) we have entertain'd the Worthy and Reverend Mr. John Garzia who (in pursuance to your Lordship's Licence) had preach'd the Gospel and Acted as a parish Minister in Virginia for nine years past; By which Licence together with a Certificate from Dr. Blear Commissary of, and Attested by the Governor of Virga. Setting forth his diligence in his function and good behaviour, And having had upwards of one and twenty months Experience, we are encourag'd to retain the said Reverend Minister; but to our extrem Grief, the maintenance that we by reason of our poverty can afford him, is far short of our inclinations in Supporting decently a man of his worth and merit.

And Whereas we were also encourag'd to retain the said Mr. John Garzia with hopes of having due provisions made for the Clergy pursuant to his Majesties Instructions to our Governor and Council, which provisions have not yet, nor is there any visible appearance of any to be made, we find our expectations therein defeated, by which means the inhabitants in general are deprived of having the Gospel preach'd amongst them and very often as well Antient, as young persons die without Baptism.

And Whereas (as well by the frequent applications of the said Reverend Mr. Garzia as our own free and earnest inclinations to carry on so good a work) we are now building at our own proper Costs a Small Church (being the only one in the whole province) but we fear that our Abilities will be far short of compleating and adorning the same as becomes the temple of God. We therefore your Petitioners most humbly pray that your Lordship (as our Diocesan) will use your best endeavours in assisting and forwarding the Petition Annext [the petition authored by Garzia which follows] and to do Such other Acts of Charity in our favour as to your Lordship shall seem meet And your Petitioners (as in duty bound) shall ever pray.

> Robt. Turner, Edward Salter, church wardens, Thos. Jewell, Wm. Willis, John Barrow, Simon Alderson, James Singellton, Charles Odeon, John Odeon

[Endorsed:]
The humble Petition of the
Church-wardens and Vestry of St. Thomas's
Parish in the province of North Carolina in America
October the 10th 1734 (Cain 353-54).

Appendix F

Letter from Garzia to Bishop of London, May 8, 1735.
To the Right Reverend Father in God Edmund Lord Bishop of London.

The Humble Petition of John Garzia Minister of St. Thomas's parish in North Carolina in America.
   Humbly Sheweth

That whereas your Petitioner hath been minister of this parish for almost three years last past, and having used my best Endeavours with the vestry and Parishioners to Undertake the building of a Brick Church (the walls and roof whereof is just now finished). And Whereas your petitioner finds the inhabitants in Generall well dispos'd to carry on so good a work, but that their disabilities must put a stop to their good intentions at least for some years. Your Petitioner therefore thinks it his bounden duty to lay this their poor Condition and willingness before your Lordship, and humbly to petition your Lordship to intercede with the Society in our behalf, in order to obtain for us the Severall necessaries annext hereto, and your Petitioner (as in duty bound) shall always pray for your Lordships Prosperity and Remain Your Lordships Most Obedient Humble Son and Servant.

John Garzia

    A Bible
2 Common Prayer Books
1 Book of Homilies
(Some Monitors against Profaneness etc.
to be distributed among my parishioners)
A Font
A pulpit Cloth and Cushion
A Carpet for the Communion table
Other conveniencies as your Lordship shall think proper (all being wanting).

[Endorsed]
The humble Petition of John Garzia Minister of St. Thomas's Parish in No. Carolina in America
May 8th 1735   (Cain 357-58).

Appendix G
Letter from Garzia to Bishop of London, May 8, 1735
May it please your Lordship.

Having been Licenced by your Lordship for about twelve years past to preach the Gospel in Virga., and having done my duty, with that Sincerity (I hope) as becomes a minister of the Establish'd English church as will appear by a Certificate from Mr. Comissary Blair, and Attested by the Governor of that colony; And having also comply'd with the instructions of the society by doctor Thomas Bray deliver'd to me in your Lordship's presence to instruct and Baptize the Negroes in Virginia; And having remov'd from thence into this province with my family in hopes to be further serviciable to the church, and the Labourers being few, and the harvest too great, appears to me to want the assistance of more of my Brethren. Notwithstanding for almost three years I have done my duty in this province not only in my own parish, but in severall others as mov'd with compassion to see them as sheep without a shepherd (as more at Large you Lordship whill be inform'd by the Governor) and all this time supporting my self and family out of the small stock I saved in Virgia. Notwithstanding the misfortune of being cast away in my passage hither, My Salary here not exceeding 24 or 25 sterling, I humbly move your Lordship (as being very willing to continue here) to intercede with the Society in my behalf, and to cause a remission to be made to the Governor as well for my past services, as for my future maintenance in consideration of my great poverty. Well remembring your Lordships Goodness to me heretofore, emboldens me to implore your charitable assistance for the future, and Conclude praying for your Lordshops health, prosperity and God's blessing; these are the wishe's of your

Lordship's Most dutiful son and most Obedient Humble Servant (Cain 358-59).

Appendix H
Letter from Garzia to SPG, May 8, 1735.
To the Right Honourble the Society for propogateing the Gospel in Foreign parts.

The Humble Petition of John Garzia Minister of St. Thomas's parish in
Beaufort precinct in North Carolina.
Humbly Sheweth.

  That your petitioner about twelve years ago was sent and licenced to preach the Gospel in Virginia, in which time your Petitioner receiv'd Instructions from your honourable board (By the hands of Doctor Thomas Bray) in order to Baptize and instruct the Negroes in that Colony. And that your petitioner pursuant thereto did (having made report thereof some years ago to the said Dr. Bray in order to be comunicated to your Board) Baptize and instruct severall Negroes as [it] appears by the List hereunto annext. And Whereas there was an allowance to have been made by your honourable Society for the same, your Petitioner therefore humbly prays, that your Honourable Board will be pleased to transmitt for the said service such an allowance As to you shall seem meet.

And your petitioner (as in duty bound) shall ever pray for your Honour's prosperity and Remain your Diligent and Most Obedient humble Servant.

                        John Garzia
    [Endorsed]
    The humble Petition of John
    Garzia Minister of St. Thomas's
    Parish in No. Carolina America

May 8th, 1735   (Cain 357).

Appendix I
Letter from Garzia to SPG, April 16, 1741.
Bath Town No. Carolina

April the 16th 1741

Sir

The 26th of May 1740 I sent a Letter to yr. Reverence by the way of South Carolina, in which in the first place I begg'd of you to offer my humble Thanks to the Honorable Society for propagating the Christian Knowledge in Forreign parts, having appointed me one of their Missionarys for this Province; and made my Report according to Order, and the Notitia Parochialis but the 7th Day of February Last I understand by a Letter from my Friend in So. Carolina, that the Ship in which my Letter for you was Sent, was taken by the Spaniards; wherefore I humbly hope, it will not be imputed to me as a Neglect of Duty; and according to Gratitude I desire the favour of you, to return my humble and hearty thanks to their Lordships and Honors the Honorable Society for having appointed me their unworthy Chaplin a Missionary for this Province; and likewise for their great Charity in appointing me Sallery for the Preceding Years. I inclose here to you my reports not only as a Missionary, but what happened between my last report and my Mission.

His Excellency orderd me according to Instructions, to fix my Residence in the Parish to which he had before Inducted me. That is to Say, at Bath Town in St. Thomas parish in the County of Beaufort. I have demanded of Mrs. Boyd Relict of my Predicessor the Books belonging to the Mission, according to order; but received only a Bible in Folio, a Common Prayer Book, the Book of Homelies and Doctor Tillotsons Sermons Three Volumes; for which I gave a Receipt, as for the rest She

139

can only say, that her Husband frequently lent them out, and all her Endeavours to find them Seem ineffectual which is a great Injury done to the distressed Widdow of a Clergyman and worthy of yr. Compassion and Notice. The Thirtyth Day of July last I received yr. Last Letter to me by order of the Society dated the 19th of November 1739 the Contents of it I communicated to his Excellency the Governor and the Assembly then Siting at Edenton, his Excellency orderd me to wait upon the Kings Attorney, one of the Members, to introduce yr. Letter to the House; which done the House orderd me to have Passage Ferry free, over the Severall Rivers and Creeks within my Mission, at the Expence of the Publick. I have read yr. Letter in the Several places I have officiated in Since, without any effect: So far (I am sorry to say it) are the People here from contributing to the Advancement of the Glory of God under the auspicious protection of the Honorable Society. Manageing in the most frugall Manner my traveling Expences will not be less than five pound Sterling per Annum in a Country where a Bale for a Horse to a Missionary is not to be had withour pay. I pray you Sir to recommend to their Lordships and honors to Send me Some Monitors against Swearing, Drunkeness, and breach of the Sabbath also preparatorys for worthyly approching the Lords Table; and if possible a few Spelling Books for the Erudition of poor Children within my Mission; and farther pray, that a Silver Cup with the Hutch and Plate of any other Proper Metal, for the decent Administring the Lords Supper, may be added, at my own Expence payable out of my Sallery, with the Name of the Donor. I recommend my Self to the prayers of our Fathers the Prelates and the rest of the Honorable Society and yr. own Reverend Sir likewise My prayers for all my Benefactors and Masters cease not as I always shall be Reverend Sir Their and your most obliged and Most humble Servant.
            John Garzia

P.S. As this Place has no direct Correspondence but to the Ports of Bristole and Liverpoole I pray an Order for making my Reports by the way of either as opportunity shall happen (Cain 420-21).

Appendix J
Notitia Parochialis from Garzia to SPG, April 16, 1741.

Notitia Parochialis
   The Report of John Garzia Missionary

	Number
The Number of Men Women and Children within my parish and Mission is computed to be	9000
Number Baptized within my Parish and Mission Since appointed Missionary	519
Adult Persons formerly Quakers	011
Actual Communicantsin my Parish Twenty Seven Within my Mission Exclusive of my parish Seventy two	099
To be more exact I refer for the Numbers of the Church of England To my next Report	
The Number of Dissenters refer'd to my next but Papists in my Parish Nine, out of my Parish yet discover'd but three	012
The number of Infidels by Information not above Two Hundred	200
Of Converts etc. Eleven	011
For Two years before I was a Missionary Baptized 247 and Three Negroes in all	250

[Addressed:]
To The Reverend Phillip Barecroft D.D.

Secretary to the Honorable Society for propagating
The Christian knowledge in forreign Parts
In Warwick Court Warwick Lane London
Per Capt. Howan for Leverpool

[Endorsed]
North Carolina
Mr. Garzia April 16, 1741 (Cain 421-22).

Notes

Spain
[1] Civita Vecchia, Italy, lies northwest of Rome on the Tyrrhenian Sea. It has served as the major port for Rome since ancient times.

Ireland
[1] The oath of Abjuration was an oath of renunciation of allegiance to James II and his issue. King James II, a Roman Catholic, was deposed by parliament in the "Glorious Revolution" of 1688-89 and the Protestants, William of Orange and Mary, assumed co-regency in February 1689.

[2] Dublin Castle which dates from the early 13th century, served as the official residence of the British chief representative, the Lord Lieutenant. Parliament and administrative offices were housed in Dublin Castle, and there were also apartments for local persons (such as Garzia) who worked in some capacity for the British administration and, additionally, for visiting kings and other dignitaries.

[3] McGrath refers to *regular* (as opposed to *secular*) priests. A regular cleric is one who is a member of a religious order whereas a secular priest is not bound by vows to a monastic or other order. Accordingly, in addition to the Archbishop of Dublin, Garzia informed on one secular and five regular priests.

[4] Very little written communication is available relating to the Garzias during their four year stay in Dublin Cas-

tle, presumably because Garzia had direct access to government officials.

[5] The Duke of Bolton, Charles Paulet, was Lord Lieutenant (head of state) of the colony of Ireland 1717-1719.

[6] An old British coin worth four pennies.

[7] This is the only mention in Irish accounts that Garzia might serve as an Anglican priest.

John Garzia, the Anglican Priest

[1] Around 1665, upon hearing the report of Dr. Thomas Bray, his commissary in Maryland, the Bishop of London, Dr. Henry Compton, persuaded King Charles II to establish the "king's bounty." This was a one-time payment of £20 to every Anglican minister or school teacher who could be persuaded to remove to the American colonies. This bonus continued well into the eighteenth century.

2 Regarding Garzia's detention in Cork, Powell cites Gerald Fothergill, A List of Immigrant Ministers to America 1690-1811, London, Elliot Stock, 1904. However Fothergill does not mention the episode of Garzia's detention., Further, a search of the Law Society Library of Ireland as well as the newspapers of the time provides no hint of any legal action against Garzia in Ireland.

Colonial Virginia

[1] The office of Episcopal Commissary, which had been in existence in England from pre-Reformation times, was instituted in order to assist a bishop to administer the farthermost reaches of his diocese. For administrative purposes the American colonies were included in the diocese of London.

² On November 10, 1878 an address entitled "An Historical Paper" was delivered by one Otto Sievers Barten at a celebration of the fiftieth anniversary of the consecration of the second structure for Christ Church, Norfolk, Virginia. The address was printed, and included in this publication was a list of the rectors who had formerly served the church and a list of those who were able to attend the celebration. "Rev'd [sic] Garzia" was listed for the year 1724 (Barten).

³ Farnham is located in Richmond County, in Virginia's "Northern Neck," the peninsula between the Potomac and Rappahannock Rivers. The town is 44 miles east of Richmond and its 2002 population was 1,356.

⁴ Daughter Mary's birth date was not recorded in the Richmond County Register. Presumably she was born prior to her family's move to Farnham from eastern Virginia..

⁵ A study of Virginia and North Carolina records reveals that, due to the scarcity of specie, debts were often paid in commodities rather than money. In Virginia and North Carolina, tobacco, and less frequently, Indian corn were the principal commodities used. Lefler writes that a law of 1715 "rated" by law sixteen commodities that were used as legal tender in colonial North Carolina (157-58).

⁶ Lefler writes that the small farmer class was by far the largest element of the colonial population. In addition to small subsistence farmers, this class also included small merchants, overseers, tavern keepers, fur traders, naval stores workers, blacksmiths, gunsmiths and workers in other industries (121).

Colonial North Carolina

[1] A new North Farnham Church was completed in 1737, four years after Garzia left Virginia. The North Farnham Episcopal Church Women write that the date of the replacement of the first North Farnham Church is given by an order of Council in October 1733, settling a dispute between "the inhabitants and vestry of that parish." The governor and council ordered "that the new church proposed by the said Vestry be built at the place already appointed (46)."

[2] There were fewer wealthy landowners in North Carolina than in neighboring colonies. Under the "headright" system of granting land which prevailed during the proprietary period, the colonial government, in most cases, followed the general policy of restricting the size of grants, with the result that North Carolina became a colony of small land-owners. Consequently less of a wealthy plantation aristocracy developed than in the neighboring colonies of Virginia and South Carolina.

Religion in Colonial North Carolina

[1] The Council was chosen by the proprietors to assist the governor in executive and administrative matters. Its members sat with the elected members of the Assembly as the legislative body. The governor was the president of the council whose number varied at times from six to twelve (Lefler 41, 66).

[2] In Quakerism's early years, Friends were persecuted and were imprisoned for refusing to take oaths. Finally, as an alternative, the right to affirm was enacted.

[3] Daniel was directly connected to colonial Bath. He lived on Archbell Point at the mouth of Bath Creek prior to his move to South Carolina.

[4] The colonial legislature later established September 22 as a day of fasting and prayer in remembrance of the massacre in Bath County in 1711.

[5] Urmstone wrote the SPG that "abundance of scandalouse, I hope false, stories are told of him; 'tis said, provided I could have been removed, he would have stay'd in this Parish and not have taken a farthing of them (which was a very endearing Article) for he had a sufficient support form Engd; if true I believe he'll be of another opinion now, for he has married a sorry girl in Virga., besides his way of living [requ]ires a good Income (Cain 209).

[6] The Reverend Mr. Thomas Gale was the brother of St. Thomas vestryman Christopher Gale of Bath, North Carolina, who had, in 1712, been appointed the first Chief Justice of the North Carolina Supreme Court.

[7] Though North Carolina was in their charge, neither Johnston nor the subsequent two Carolina commissaries, ever made a visit from their homes in Charleston, South Carolina to North Carolina.

[8] Notwithstanding their descriptions of North Carolina by colonial clergymen (Cain xli, 27, 29-30, 233), the SPG, the Bishop of London and other European institutions were unable to conceive of the extent of wilderness and geographic enormity of the New World and (during early settlement) its lack of infrastructure such as roads and bridges.

Bath Town

[1] A glebe is a plot of land belonging to or yielding revenue to a parish or ecclesiastical benefice. The St. Thomas glebe was located south of Glebe Creek near Archbell Point at the mouth of Bath Creek.

² This is the oldest church in use in North Carolina. Presumably because the builders did not have access to surveying instruments of that era, the building was constructed several feet out of square, and it was located directly in the right of way for Craven Street.

³ The Garzia home was located on lots, numbers 49, 50 and 51 (as originally numbered by John Lawson and his partners.) The property was on the west side of King Street, an extension of Edenton Road, the route of entry into and out of Bath Town in the colonial period. Coincidentally, this is the same location of the residence of a twentieth century rector of St. Thomas Church, Bath. (See map, page 92.)

⁴ The land amounted to 280 acres and was located on the east side of South Creek. It is listed as "in Beaufort on the East side of the South Dividing Creek (South Creek), joining the side of the creek Swamp, the Pocoson, and the Main run at the head of Tarripin gut" (Hoffman 4).

⁵ For example: the 1715 "Act Concerning Servants and Slaves" required churchwardens to sell the service of female servants who bore a child by their master, or of any white woman who did so by a Negro, Mulatto, or Indian. The proceeds were to go to the parish vestry. Likewise the children of any such unions were to be bound out, and the vestry received any profits from the transaction.

⁶ These taxes were widely resented, not only by Quakers and other "dissenters," but also by many Anglicans. Resistance to this kind of taxation was, perhaps, one of the reasons for the establishment clause in the First Amendment of the U.S. Constitution.

⁷ Unfortunately a portion of these savings was someway lost in "the misfortune of being cast away in my passage hither" (Cain 359).

[8] The letter from the St. Thomas Vestry to the Bishop of London was written October 10, 1734, however it was not until May 8, 1735 that it was included with the mailing of a letter from Garzia to the SPG and letters from Garzia to the Bishop of London.

[9] Presumably this letter accompanied those letters of the same date addressed to Bishop of London Gibson.

[10] Paper money issued by the provincial government (Lefler 157).

[11] In a footnote, Cain relates that when Garzia's letter was presented at the meeting of the SPG, the secretary stated that the two previous petitions had not been received and that he, the secretary, did not know Garzia. The letter to the Bishop of London was then presented and acted upon (Cain 366).

[12] As far as is known, Mr. Garden never visited North Carolina though the most important duty of the commissaries was to report on the state of their districts and especially the conditions of the clerics therein (Cain xliv).

[13] On taking up his duties in the southern half of the province, Mr. Moir soon realized that it was impossible to fully comply with his charged duties. He wrote the Secretary that

> this part of the Province where I am Missionary is about 150 miles in breadth along the coast and that in some places they have settled upwards of 150 miles back from the sea. The Inhabitants are very much scattered, and most of them live at a great distance from one another which renders it impossible for me to serve them as I could wish. The gener-

149

ality of them are extremely ignorant (Cain 408-09).

[14] This letter was directed to St. Paul's Parish because most of the provincial legislative sessions were being held in Edenton at that time.

[15] Some of the present residents of Bath are pleased to note that the curse appears to have taken.

[16] A *notitia parochialis* is a formal ecclesiastical report which lists the clerics activities, such as numbers of communicants, number of persons baptized, etc. for a specified period of time.

[17] The chalice is still a proud possession of St. Thomas Church, Bath (Angley 52).

[18] Mary Garzia was, likely, the teacher for her children and probably encouraged her husband to seek shipments of educational materials. During the Revolution their son, John was commissioned an officer and paymaster in the Continental Army which suggests he was a fairly well-educated man.

Epilogue

[1] King George's War — the American phase of the Austrian Succession, 1744 - 1748 – one of the four "French and Indian Wars" — the American historical designation for the colonial wars between Great Britain and France.

[2] St. Thomas Parish was without a priest during the nine years between the ministries of John Garzia and Alexander Stewart.

Appendix

[1] In present-day calendars the date given in the nun's trial would read February 6, 1719 instead of 1718. During the twelfth century England adopted the "Year of Grace"

calendar. This calendar began the new year on March 25, as opposed to January 1. The former date was traditionally regarded by English Christians as the day of the Conception of Christ with nine months passage to the Nativity on December 25. All days from January 1 through March 24 belonged to the previous year. However, to the further confusion of modern historians, a calendar year starting on January 1 was used for almanacs and various other official purposes. To avoid ambiguity, some authors show the date from January 1 through March 24 with both calendar styles. *(e.g.* The nun's trial would be dated February 6, 1718/19). In Great Britain the day of the start of the year was officially changed to January 1 by the same Act of Parliament that adopted the Gregorian Calendar in 1752.

[2] The correct date is 1719 (Cain 187n).

Works Cited

Angley, Wilson. A History of St. Thomas Episcopal Church, Bath, North Carolina. Raleigh: Division of Archives and History. NC Dept. Cultural Re sources, 1981.

Barten, Otto Sievers. An Historical Paper." Read at the Fiftieth Aniversary of the Consecration of the Present Building of Christ Church, Norfolk, VA., on Sunday, November 10th , 1878. Norfolk: Virginian Job, 1878.

Beaufort County Deed Book. Beaufort County Court house, Washington, NC.

Brydon, George M. Virginia's Mother Church and the Political Conditions Under Which It Grew. 2 vols. Richmond, VA: Virginia Historical Society, 1947.

Burke, William. The Irish Priests in the Penal Times, Shannon, Ireland: Irish University Press, 1968.

Cain, Robert, ed. The Church of England in North Carolina: Documents, 1599-1741. The Colonial Records of North Carolina. Second Series, 10 Vol. Raleigh: N Dept. of Cultural Resources, 1999.

Drysdale, Hugh. "Hugh Drysdale to Bishop of London, Williamsburg, 10 July 1724": Virginia Colonial Records Project. Microfilm reel 591, 90. Rich mond: Library of Virginia.

Hahn, Emily. Fractured Emerald: Ireland. Garden City, NY: Doubleday, 1971.

Hawks, Francis. History of North Carolina From 1663 to 1729. Vol. 2. Fayetteville, NC: Hale, 1858. 2 vols.

Hofman, Margaret, Colony of North Carolina, Abstracts of Land Patents,1735 - 1764, Vol. 1. Weldon, NC: Roanoke News, 1978. 2 vols.

King, George H.S., ed. The Registers of North Farnham Parish 1663-1814 and Lunenburg Parish 1783-1800. Fredericksburg, VA: George King, 1966.

Laws in Ireland for the Suppression of Popery commonly known as the Penal Laws. Ed. Patricia Schaffer. 2000. U of MN Law School. 27 Jan 2003. <http://www.las.umn.edu/irishlaw/indcx.html>

Lefler, Hugh T., and Albert R. Newsome. North Carolina. Chapel Hill, NC: U of NC, 1954.

MacGrath, Kevin. "John Garzia, a Noted Priest-catcher and His Activities, 1717-23." The Ecclesiastical Record 72 (1949): 506-14.

Manross, William Wilson, ed. The Fulham Papers in the Lambeth Palace Library, American Colonial Section Calendar and Indexes Oxford: Clarendon Press. 1965

McKendrick, Melveena. Spain. New York: American Heritage, 1972.

.New Revised Standard Version Bible. New York: Harper, 1989.

North Farnham Episcopal Church Women. North Farnham Parish, 1683-1991. Farnham, VA: North Farnham Episcopal Church, 1991.

Powell, William, ed. Dictionary of North Carolina Biography. Vol 2, Chapel Hill: U of NC P., 1979. 6 vols.

Rhode Island USGen Web. Genealogy and History Project. Ed. Susan Pieroth. 6 Sept. 2002. US Gen Web. 15 Nov.2002 <http://www.rootsweb.com/~rigerweb/ >.

Saunders, William, ed. The Colonial Records of North Carolina, 1734-1752. Vol. IV. New York: AMS Press, 1968. 26 vols.

Sparacio, Ruth and Sam Sparacio. eds. Richmond County, Virginia, Order Books 1721-1732 and 1732- 1739). McLean VA: Antient, 1998.

Wake Letters. Vol. 13. (1718). Oxford, England: Christ Church Library. 31 vols.

Wall, Maureen. The Penal Laws 1691-1760. Dundalk, Ireland: Dundalgan, 1967.

To order copies of
The Lives and Times of John Garzia

Check with your local bookstore or complete and mail the form below

....

I want _____ copies of *The Lives and Times of John Garzia* for $~~22.00~~ 19.95 each.

For handling and shipping include $4.00 for one book and $2.00 for each additional book. (For shipment outside the United States, add $8.00 for one book and $4.00 for each additional book.)

My check or money order for $ _____ is enclosed.

Name_____

Address_____

_____

City_____

State/Zip_____

Make your check or money order payable and return to

Historic Bath
P.O. Box 148
Bath, NC 27808

Profits from the sale of this volume benefit the Historic Bath State Historic Site